ME, HER AND TWO DOGS

Living the dream... sort of

By

Elizabeth Larkswood

To E. Thank you for your love and support.

CONTENTS

Introduction *1*
Chapter 1 .... *3*
Chapter 2 .... *8*
Chapter 3 .... *14*
Chapter 4 .... *19*
Chapter 5 .... *22*
Chapter 6 .... *26*
Chapter 7 .... *37*
Chapter 8 .... *40*
Chapter 9 .... *44*
Chapter 10 .... *48*
Chapter 11 .... *54*
Chapter 12 .... *60*
Chapter 13 .... *67*
Chapter 14 .... *76*
Chapter 15 .... *82*
Chapter 16 .... *87*
Chapter 17 .... *93*
Chapter 18 .... *97*
Chapter 19 .... *103*
Chapter 20 .... *109*
Chapter 21 .... *115*
Chapter 22 .... *120*
Chapter 23 .... *124*
Chapter 24 .... *129*
Chapter 25 .... *137*
Chapter 26 .... *143*
Chapter 27 .... *150*
Chapter 28 .... *155*
Chapter 29 .... *162*
Chapter 30 .... *167*
Chapter 31 .... *173*
Chapter 32 .... *178*

Chapter 33...*185*
Chapter 34...*189*
Chapter 35...*193*
Chapter 36...*199*
Chapter 37...*204*
Chapter 38...*209*
About The Author...*215*

ACKNOWLEDGMENTS

*To the wonderful people of Wales for your sense of humour,
your kindness and your acceptance.*

INTRODUCTiON

I was asked to publish a daily blog by our friends and family after my partner Helen and I decided to retire from our professional lives in the NHS – me as a nurse, her as a podiatrist – and buy a house with land in Wales. We had a need to live our dream, grow our own vegetables and for Helen to immerse herself in her garden. We had holidayed every year in Wales and it had become our second home to a large extent; the next natural step for us was to make it our permanent home. The blog became this book with additions.

The last five years of our lives had been dreadful. Helen had undergone treatment for breast cancer in 2011 and thankfully is clear now. Her sister Daphne, aged sixty-three, was diagnosed the following year with primary peritoneal cancer. She came to live with us after diagnosis so we could nurse her for the little time she had left and within seven months she had passed away. Three days after her death I was diagnosed with rheumatoid arthritis.

My elderly mother had been living with us for fourteen years and her mental health started to decline due to vascular dementia. We had lost three dogs all to cancer, two ten weeks apart. After Daphne died Helen's father, who had previously been cared for by her sister, suffered a decline in his health quite rapidly due to grief, I am sure, resulting in him no longer being able to manage on his own, and he came to live with us. After I retired on ill-health grounds we decided to buy a house in West Sussex to be near where Helen worked. My mother's mental health declined rapidly to the point where I could no longer leave her for any period of time and the situation became untenable; the feelings of failure I had exacerbated by the fact that I was a nurse were overpowering but I was fortunate enough that her social worker found her a lovely care home. Shortly after this Helen's father died, and just two weeks before our move to Wales my mum fell and subsequently received a brain haemorrhage and developed pneumonia, and I literally held her funeral five days before we moved.

CHAPTER 1

The removal manager stood in the kitchen of our old house in a posh suit with a posh voice and reassured me I needed his company's services because of my previous hideous experiences, and that with his company our move to Wales would be seamless. His company, he said, had a branch in Swansea; a team of men would meet the two chaps driving down all our worldly goods and the whole process would run like clockwork.

I believed him.

The whole job was to take a week with a 'team' of men coming on the Monday to start the packing and loading, returning on the Tuesday to leave us with the bare essentials and then Wednesday, moving day, we would be out before we knew it. On arrival the 'team' from Swansea would meet us at the property and everything would be a positive experience from start to finish.

I believed him.

We had found, after searching for over a year, our dream cottage in the countryside in Carmarthenshire. It was the quintessential chocolate box house, built in 1840. An acre of land surrounded it on both sides; this was full of trees, hornbeams, white willows, silver birch, all standing in an enormous lawned area and borders stacked with various plants. A large stream flowed through part of it and to crown it all a dovecote, built in 1760, stood proudly in the back of the garden near the vegetable plot which was to be my domain. It was beautiful. It was in a valley with far-reaching views of hills and forests. Our nearest neighbour was across the private lane we were situated on but not visible from our cottage; the other neighbour was about two hundred yards further down the lane. We were overjoyed with our find, especially as we had lost two other houses through no fault of our own and thought we would never match them. This cottage turned out to be better than both, proving that all good things come to those who wait.

So the first day of our moving week arrived. We got up bright and early awaiting 'the team' but unfortunately due to traffic they would be delayed and arrive about half past nine. Never mind, these things happen, we told ourselves.

So the team arrived, and I use the term loosely as it consisted of just two men. One who was mainly to do the packing and the other was coming with us to Wales as he was the driver. I shall call them Packer and Driver for the sake of this narrative.

So Driver goes upstairs to start packing the forty pairs of shoes that Helen owns and the multitude of clothes she possesses. In fairness a lot of these clothes were her sister's but it's fair to say she does have a clothing and shoe fetish regardless.

Meantime, Packer starts in the kitchen. If it wasn't nailed down it was going in a box and even if it was nailed down it may well be jemmied into submission and end up in a box anyway. I actually found him at one point packing a half-eaten lemon drizzle cake in a plastic cake container. He seemed very surprised when I asked him to leave the cake out so we could actually eat it.

The speed at which he packed was phenomenal, frighteningly so. I ended up surreptitiously trying to spy on him and counting the dogs to make sure they were still there. We have two dogs, by the way. Flo, a boxer, soft as butter and an attention seeker. Phoebe is of uncertain origin but came to us via Greece as she is a rescue dog. Both girls are the same age and inseparable. Phoebe we think has pointer or foxhound origins as she stalks birds, squirrels, you name it, Phoebe stalks it; even a half-stuffed grey corduroy hippo with no legs gets the instinctive Phoebe treatment.

The Packer and the Driver left at four thirty after copious

amounts of tea, cakes and biscuits and said they would try to be earlier the next day. We were not impressed but Helen and I are quite positive-thinking people and tried to keep our spirits up.

The next day three men! Three men arrived! In my opinion it barely passes as a team but as I was losing the will to live I felt stupidly grateful we had actually improved by one whole person.

The van started to be loaded and slowly but surely the house started to empty. Up until now I had always considered the home to be pristine. Not so. Once all furniture and pictures, rugs and ornaments have been removed all the crap shows. Out came the emulsion and Polyfilla, followed closely by the spray bleach. We fell into bed that night exhausted. Even my eyelashes hurt but we were buoyed by the big day approaching and felt encouraged as our last night arrived, and were keeping everything crossed, albeit painfully, for a smooth move to Wales the next day.

All we were left with was our bed, the dogs' beds and just a few items that still needed packing. The removal men didn't leave that day until about six o'clock. I couldn't sleep, Helen couldn't sleep, but by the law of sod we both drifted off at around half past five in the morning and overslept. Stupidly lulled into thinking the excitement of the move would ensure us waking early, we didn't set an alarm. It was a quarter to eight when we did wake up and we stumbled out of bed knowing the removal men were due in fifteen minutes.

Two men arrived, Driver and the third man. Both terrific, hardworking men who did everything they could to give us a 'seamless' experience as promised by posh manager man, but it didn't happen, it couldn't because it was just the two of them and there was only so much they could do in a given space of time. The management team let us and them down badly. I fell for his patter. There really is no fool like an old fool.

The van left at ten o'clock and we finished off the cleaning and ensured all keys were lined up on the kitchen work surface, clearly labelled, then after having said goodbye to our neighbours we finally got in our cars for the four and a half hour drive to our new life. I was to follow Helen's car. I had picked up my mum's ashes the day before and sat her in the front seat next to me with the seat belt wrapped around the dark red carrier bag containing the dark red cardboard box, which contained all that was left of part of my heart.

The journey to Wales was uneventful apart from the very painful bladder syndrome you always get when you know you can't actually access a loo easily. We kept in contact via our hands-free phones so Helen and I were able to speak often. I watched Flo in the back of Helen's car staring back at me, bemused as to why Phoebe and I were following them. We stopped after two hours for me to find a loo and Helen to have a Costa coffee to keep her alive and with a pulse. The dogs peed too so all was well... or so we thought.

About halfway through our journey we received a phone call to say that the cottage was officially ours and completion had taken place. Great news! However, the next phone call was from our vendor's estate agents to tell us they would not be finished moving out until mid-afternoon. Not to worry, we said, we won't be there until about half past three anyway. As it turned out it was four o'clock and by then pitch black and raining heavily. We had never wanted to move in the winter. We had put our house on the market in March to hopefully ensure a summer move... What folly! After losing two houses due to all the things that can go wrong during this ridiculous, painful, archaic process, going wrong, we ended up with Hobsons' choice and a winter move it was.

We arrived at the estate agents to pick up the keys only to find they had not been dropped off yet so we decided to drive to the cottage only to pass the vendors on their way to drop off the keys at the estate agents we had just left. After exchanging pleasantries in the pouring rain we finally got to open the door of our new home.

Having had the foresight to ensure we had the kettle, tea, milk etc. we were able to sustain ourselves until three hours later when our furniture arrived. The rain by now was torrential and as there are no street lights the van stayed at the end of the lane as it is narrow and the driver was unsure if he could get as far as our house. However, assured by his co-worker that he could get part of the way, we stood in the rain and cold watching whilst the lorry slowly, inch by inch, made its way nearer and nearer to us and got to our gate. We decided that all that was needed that night was our bed, so eventually, the bed in situ, the men went off to find somewhere to park and sleep overnight in the purpose-built cabin these huge lorries have for this very situation.

We did sleep this night and so did the dogs, which was a worry we had both had, but they must have been as tired as us and having been fed and watered and their familiar bedding laid down for them, they seemed content and happy, a bit like us two.

CHAPTER 2

The men arrived and after being fed scrambled eggs and toast they set to work. They were stupidly grateful we fed them! I really cannot believe that they were surprised I offered them food. Evidently they never get fed by the people they are moving. What do the these customers think these poor blokes exist on for a week? They went on to tell me that on an away job such as this one, most of any overtime or extra money earned is spent on feeding themselves at café prices.

They worked like stink. And to top it all, Mr Posh Manager Man had rung and given them another job to do on their way home and even suggested they tried to finish our move today instead of tomorrow. I was starting to get a little cross by now (said the master of understatement) and eventually rang Mr Posh Manager Man and explained to him my exact feelings about his management skills and his integrity regarding the promises he makes to trusting, paying customers. I also reminded him that reviews on social media sites are read and asked him what he thought I should write. I gave him a gob full, a very controlled, assertive, non-sweary gob full. It will make no difference to Mr Posh Manager but I certainly felt better and I could tell by the grins on our removal men's faces, who had overheard some of the exchange, that they felt vindicated also.

The day got longer and longer, the cottage got messier and messier, and at nine o'clock the men had actually finished. The only room we could actually call partially habitable was one bedroom, the kitchen and half the lounge. One bedroom resembled a screenshot from Tetris with every possible shaped box crammed in to fit.

During this day we had a visit from our neighbour, the one down the lane. A beautiful human being called Trevor, he has the most wonderful broad Welsh accent and almost sings his way through each conversation. We had to admit to each other after he had left that we didn't understand some of his conversation but he came to ask if we needed any wood for the log burner, any food, and when he found out I was hoping to keep chickens, he offered me three of his. Blown away by this stranger's friendliness and generosity this experience gave another lovely layer to what was already proving to be our dream becoming a reality.

I think I would be foolish to believe that after everything that has happened in the last few weeks that sleep would come easily every night.

In the two weeks before this move I had I spent up to seven hours a day with Mum at the hospital; fortunately we were able to get her back to her wonderful care home two days before she died where she was looked after beautifully and I am indebted to those amazing women who looked after her for the rest of my life.

I then had to arrange the funeral and I even made the flowers for the coffin because I knew all Mum's favourite flowers and colours and I wanted it to be one of the last things I could do for her.

Mingled in with all this was the exchange and subsequent mayhem that followed.

So, going to bed exhausted is clearly not enough to guarantee a good night's rest, quite the opposite. Every time I shut my eyes the events of the last few weeks started a re-run in my head. It was like Groundhog Day without the jokes.

We spent the next day trying to make some sense of the multitude of boxes and trying to put together a home that we could relax in.

What surprises me above all is the enormous amount of paper that is used when packing. This paper is like the white drawing paper you were given at school, in my day at least, and there were reams of it. I have since discovered that if you roll this paper up into sausage shapes they make the best fire starters. Therefore we are now the proud owners of enough paper fire starters to last us until Helen's 97th birthday in 2055. Bring a bottle.

Wearily we worked all day and gained a bedroom that actually looked like a bedroom, a kitchen that had things in the cupboards and a walk-in larder that I am actually in love with, a sentence I never thought I would write, and not forgetting three quarters of a living room. I actually mastered how to make a decent log fire in the burner, in fact so successfully the living room's temperature and the surface of the sun actually were at the same level Celsius at one point.

Another day of being very busy but we had time to look at our surroundings and pinch ourselves that we actually lived here amongst the hills and fields and abundance of birds. I stopped and looked at the sky and a red kite circled overhead, occasionally mobbed by crows that were attempting to escort it off the premises but not succeeding. I didn't blame it for wanting to stay. The weather had started to turn cold, that type of cold that heralds snow and as we awoke the next morning the premise of snow was a reality and if possible everything looked even more beautiful than before.

Usually in Worthing on a Saturday, Helen manages to find an excuse to either go to the 'large Tesco' in Durrington or if she really needs a proper fix for her long-standing addiction she takes herself off to Holmbush where she can get a better quality hit.

However, a very different experience awaited her and as I drove the two and a half miles to the builders' merchants (yes, you read that right) and passed three cars, I wondered with trepidation if withdrawal symptoms would kick in and I would end up frantically searching for a 'proper shop' to stop her shakes and sweats. I needn't have worried. Gareth was the man of the hour. A quietly spoken gentleman who endeavoured to find us the best deals on everything we needed. What we needed was 300ft of chicken wire to attach to the existing wooden fence to stop Flo and Phoebe rampaging through West Wales and causing havoc, and at worst ending up being shot by some well within his rights sheep farmer!

When we asked Gareth for a companion set for our fire, i.e. brush, poker, shovel etc. he informed us that there was some at his other shop in Lampeter and he would go get it and we could pick it up from his house that evening! He invited us to open an account and told us of a chap who would sort the fence out for us. He also told us that it never snows here. As he was speaking I found my gaze drifting off towards the window wondering what the white, cold stuff was all over the place but, who am I to argue? We left without parting with any money and clutching the phone number for Fred the Fencer.

I rang Fred the Fencer when we got in and arranged for him to visit Monday, stressing it was urgent... I have since come to learn that urgent here is within the next two weeks.

So we had until Fred arrived a potential escape plot problem being hatched by the dogs every time we let them out. In our infinite wisdom we decided when we got home that if Helen stood one side of our garden and I stood the other we could head off the dogs, preventing them from going behind the cottage where the gaps in the fence were, and therefore allow them off the lead to run with abandonment. Flo and Phoebe hurled themselves around the garden at breakneck speed. It warmed the cockles of my heart to see them so free and happy, that was until Flo spotted the 100ft gap that separated Helen and I and they both flew past us heading for infinity and beyond. Fortunately they were more interested in the stream that runs through our garden than the gaps in the fence and we managed, after running in circles for five minutes shouting, 'Treat!' and, 'Cheese!' to catch them.

At this point Trevor, our lovely neighbour, was feeding his one sheep and several geese and invited us to see his 'garden'. His 'garden' was three and a half acres and amazing. Broken up into woodland areas, formal flower beds and vegetable plots, it was a wonderful walk around with our new friend listening to all the hard work he and his wife Jill had put into this land between them. We discussed the best tractor mower to buy, what crops grow well in this soil and left clutching armfuls of swede, kale and a very large marrow. Then within minutes of arriving home, Trevor arrived at ours with a large frozen ham and joint of pork for our freezer. So with me being vegetarian and Helen being a carnivore we both got a meal or three from this lovely man. The kindness of this stranger is overwhelming.

I lived in Worthing for three years and never felt part of it. After three days here I felt I was home.

Wales, I love you. We both feel blessed and every now and then we look at each other and the look is like the one kids have on Christmas Eve, knowing tomorrow is going to bring joy.

*

Thicker snow had fallen overnight and was still falling in large flakes, covering the ground even further and dazzling us with its pure whiteness. Flo and Phoebe did not know what to make of it, they hared around the garden with absolute lunacy pasted across their faces. If dogs can laugh manically they did, a lot.

The surrounding countryside looked exquisite, coated in a white stillness that made even the most sparse of bushes take on a whole new beauty. The birds were diving in and out of the hedgerows trailing snowflakes in their wake, desperate for the food on the feeders and bird tables we had put out as a priority to ensure they could survive another day and night in this frozen environment that had suddenly been forced upon them.

Our Sundays are imbedded in routine. On goes Radio 4 to listen to the Archers omnibus, followed by Desert Island Discs. These are our two Sunday morning ritualistic must-hears. Even though we listen to the Archers every night, for some reason we also have to hear it again on Sunday. Helen scoffed at me when we first met for listening but is now as hooked as I am.

We decided it was time for the unpacking of the clothes. Gulp! Reader, please be aware we are not speaking of a couple of suitcases here. Imagine a stock room filled with a cross between John Lewis, M&S, Debenhams and Primark women's wear and you have the perfect image of the contents of the boxes upon boxes of Helen's haute couture. Not being able to face it, I left her to sort it out. I'm not one to colour code my clothes or hang all the trousers together. Mine tend to end up looking like the sale rail in Oxfam only messier.

I decided to try and clean the conservatory and bring some order to it. We have been using this to put the dogs in when anyone comes, feed them, and also it's been an access to get out to the garden; all of this has culminated in the floor resembling a pond when the liner has sprung a leak.

Being the sad individual I am I enjoyed this spring clean, or should I say depth of winter clean, and the room looked very organised and pristine when I had finished.

At this juncture you need some background information to enable the next little anecdote to make sense.

We have an antique old pine wardrobe. A triple one. Unfortunately we could not get it to fit in the bedroom as the little feet on it need to be removed. However, all was not lost as it is easily disassembled. The top comes off, the whole bottom with drawers and the sides and doors can be removed. Helen, in her infinite wisdom decided to put it together so at least we could hang clothes in it; this meant leaving the top bit off but just having the sides and doors on the base. I was heavily immersed in cleaning and mopping when I heard a small but desperate voice saying, 'Hannah, Han, can you help me?'

Dropping mop and climbing the stairs, I went into the bedroom that was the last place I had seen her. She wasn't there, so in confusion I wandered back onto the landing only to hear her voice again. 'Han, I'm in here.' Turning around and going back into the bedroom, I happened to notice a little tuft of grey hair peeking above the wardrobe door. She had locked herself in the wardrobe. In her efforts to get the sides and doors on she had stood on the base and lifted them up in order to position them in the right place. Unfortunately the door had shut and left her on the inside, trapped. I'd like to say something like this was an unusual occurrence but she does seem to end up in countless 'pickles', as she calls them.

The day ended with all of the available hanging space hanging things and my allocated wardrobe colour coded with all the trousers hung together... it won't last long.

CHAPTER 3

There was no snow overnight as we woke up to another day but a beautiful jigsaw puzzle blue sky and thick frozen snow underfoot. All seemed right with the world when we ran the dogs first thing that morning. Everything was wonderful and wonderful it was until I ran the taps in the kitchen only to find the sink not draining. No matter, I thought, I possess a sink plunger which just so happened to be out of its box and under the sink.

Positioning the plunger over the plughole I plunged, and then I plunged again, only to find that the clear water that would not drain was now turning a dreadful poo colour with a bouquet to match.

Desperately thinking that the more I plunged the better things would get I started to realise that the sink had a life of its own and was regurgitating the contents of its bowels back at me. Helen entered the kitchen oblivious to my plight until she came over to the sink to wash her hands and then fled in terror to the bathroom, leaving me and the sink full of putrid water alone.

I stared at it for ages hoping by some miracle it would decide to retreat back to the depths of hell from whence it came but alas, it remained content to keep me company.

I rang a couple of 'emergency' plumbers who sucked in through their teeth when I suggested I may need a visit the same day. The earliest they said would be after Christmas???? Given no choice I rand Dynorod; £145 would be the charge and they would get to us at twelve thirty. It was nine o'clock. Grateful for small mercies, I agreed and waited.

At twelve fifteen there was a knock on the door and I opened it fully expecting Dynorod Man but there stood our archangel Trevor resplendently dressed in a daft Christmas reindeer bobble hat. Behind him stood Dynorod Man.

Trevor: 'What's wrong?'

Me: 'The kitchen sink is full of poo-type watery stuff and won't drain.'

Trevor: 'Why didn't you ask me? I have all the rods and everything.'

I suddenly became aware that Dynorod Man was looking a tad confused so I invited them both in and pointed to the sink and armed with a Henry Wet and Dry vacuum Dynorod Man advanced upon the problem.

Trevor: 'Next time if you have a problem come and get me.' He looked hurt.

I found myself apologising to him for not bothering him.

Trevor: 'Right. Get your coat on and boots and meet me outside.'

I wondered at this point if we were going to have a stand-up fight and felt that at around six foot four and roughly sixteen stone he might have a small advantage over me. I duly dressed to find Trevor peering down our cess pit and when he saw me he started to explain how the sewage system of our house works. He then continued.

Trevor: 'You are getting ripped off big time and I could do it for nothing.'

This man was genuinely upset that we hadn't felt we could ask him to clear our blocked sink. I again apologised profusely and promised him I would never, ever, ask anyone else ever again to do anything apart from him, ever.

Whilst we were still in the garden Dynorod Man left saying all was well and clear, and as he drove off Trevor and I stood and waved to him, smiling as we did so.

'Bastard,' said Trevor.

Helen and I decided to check out Llanfwr, our local town. She needed the bank and we thought we would get a feel for the place that would soon become so familiar to us. After having bleached the sink and settled the dogs we got in the car and drove the 8.8 miles through winding roads that cut through white fields and snow-capped hills. More red kite circled overhead and sheep stared at us as we drove past, their coats still bearing the remnants of ice from the snowfall the day before.

Llanfwr is a picturesque town full of little shops selling wool and handmade jumpers, kitchenware, butchers displaying black Welsh beef in their shop windows. Bistros scattered around and intermingled with traditional pubs and in the middle proudly stood the Town Hall. I felt like I was in Trumpton.

When Helen was dealing with her bank business and holding up the queue for ages I noticed not one person rolled their eyes or tutted. Instead of that they chatted amongst themselves and it transpired one of the queuers was the father of the bank teller so lots of banter was pinging backwards and forwards. They looked at me whilst they spoke as a gesture of inclusion and they made me feel like a local person, known for ages to them.

On the drive home we remarked how lovely the town was and above all, friendly. No surprises there.

We had been back home about ten minutes when there was a knock on the door. It was another neighbour, David. He came in and we all introduced ourselves. Trevor had told me about David. It transpires he was a professor of forensic pathology up until his semi-retirement. He had come over to say how sorry he was we had to pay out for the plumber this morning and he had written down four pages of useful local people who could do all manner of things should we need them. On the list amongst many others were the wood merchant, the local builder, a fencer, GP, dentist, hospital, pharmacy and the like. He also gave us two tickets for free admission into the National Botanic Gardens of Wales and a potted history of the estate we lived on. He already knew we were interested in the acre of land abutting our property, one we had earmarked for an apiary and conservation area. Evidently were are not alone in our quest. Trevor wants it, he wants some of it and Lewis the farmer also would pitch in a bid for it.

When David left, Helen and I decided we would not be entering into a bidding war on a piece of land but did take on board that it would add substantial value to our house if we ever wanted to sell.

Later, as promised Fred the Fencer arrived to estimate the cost of the additional fencing we needed to dog-proof the garden. Again he was lovely and friendly and in between cracking jokes and saying he could do the job on the 25th of this month (December), it was arranged he would be able to fit us in midway through January, before if possible. He also took back all the wire we had bought from Gareth and the tacks to exchange them for stock wire fencing which he said would be more appropriate. He would get it for us and stick it on our account.

Before we moved we were secretly worried that being a same-sex couple and being English would be a problem to some people here in Wales in the middle of nowhere. Despite our belief that we deserved, like everyone else, a right to love and marry if we wanted to, we still were aware of ongoing homophobia and the rumours about the Welsh hating the English. So far so good.

One of the spare bedrooms, the Tetris room as previously mentioned, had got away with being crammed to the rafters with boxes long enough and so Helen advanced upon it like an Amazonian warrior… Well, not actually an Amazonian warrior, more sloth-like and dragging herself slowly up the stairs in a worn-out stupor.

I on the other hand felt the garage needed organising and I also couldn't find my electric drill and bits. It's what any sixty-four-year-old woman longs for, isn't it?

The removal men had basically chucked everything that didn't have a definite home in the garage. To be fair this may have been due to me repeating the phrase, 'In the garage,' every time I was asked, 'Where do you want this put, love?'

I opened the double doors of the chamber of horrors and looked at the devastation moving from Worthing to Wales and unloading in the semi-dark had left. In addition to the never-ending boxes were garden furniture, ladders, plastic boxes of Helen's dad's tools and miscellaneous stuff that had not been used for the last thirty years and by my reckoning will never be used again but we won't throw it away as it may come in handy one day.

I decided the best tactic was to firstly make enough space for me to get in the door. Always a good idea, I thought. It actually turned out to be quite a satisfying task. After about two hours of pushing and shoving the garage actually looked acceptably tidy. I went back into the cottage to see how Helen was getting on tackling the Tetris room, fully expecting to find her fast asleep on the landing.

I got to the bottom of the stairs and found the whole of the stairs covered in flattened boxes and stacked about four feet high. She had done brilliantly! The Tetris room had a floor and walls! I never knew.

By mid-afternoon we had got to the point where we could put up the spare bed. It's a heavy old oak one and has the headboard and footboard attached by two wooden struts each side that bolt on, and another that runs through the middle. Side struts duly found, however, it appeared the middle bit and bolts were missing. The next hour consisted of us pulling the house to bits to find a six-foot-long wooden strut with heavy nuts and bolts taped to it. The newly tidied garage got another once over but to no avail.

Time to phone the removal company. They must rue the day I hired them. I was put through to anther manager and after explaining about the missing bed bit he telephoned the driver and the second removal man but neither of them knew where they had put it. Great. Love it when things go so smoothly.

We are going to pull the garage and shed to bits tomorrow to ensure the piece isn't hiding in them, sniggering at us every time we walk past or open the doors to stare into the vast area of junk scratching our heads in bewilderment.

CHAPTER 4

I have discovered that there is a certain place in the bathroom upstairs that if you place the scales you weigh roughly four pounds less than your actual weight and don't even have to stand on one leg. The scales are staying there regardless of health and safety.

Talking of weight, we have been a bit worried about Flo. She never seems to put on weight and she has had a couple of wee accidents in the house. Something Flo never has done since she was a puppy. So both of us Googled all the symptoms and came up with an extensive list of what was wrong with her and top of that was diabetes.

The veterinary system here is very different to what we are used to. I had already registered both dogs prior to moving with a practice in Llanfwr, and it just so happened we parked outside it the other day when we went there. The vets offer open clinics on a first come first served basis and we knew they were open every day for half an hour every afternoon. So we both decided we needed a wee sample. Helen had found a cheap plastic watering can that instead of a spout had an open trough-like aperture attached to it. So there we were armed with watering jug following Flo around the garden, waiting for that all telling squat. Helen was brilliant at this. We managed to get, over three trips out, enough wee to be dipped by the vet and decanted it into one of my specimen pots.

As it wasn't until the afternoon we still had to look for the bed thingy otherwise the line-up of people wanting to visit us would not have a bed.

Helen found it propped up in the garage in the corner by the door with nuts and bolts attached. It was metal and I had been looking for a wooden strut for some reason best known to myself.

After a lot of moving this over there and that over here the bed took shape and with one almighty heave the heaviest mattress in the world landed on the bed frame. So, future guests, you will not have to sleep on the floor. All is well. I sheepishly phoned the removal company and in my best pathetic voice apologised. They were gracious in their acceptance and I never want to speak to them again. The is a particular stone in the garden I shall crawl under if I ever have to.

Time for the vets. The heavens opened, the wind blew. Torrential rain descended upon us. Each time we let the dogs out, the preparation to get out and then return took longer than the actual event. Muddy wellies, scarves, already damp coats and an assortment of really stupid-looking hats accompanied this soggy occurrence. Oh, joy.

Flo was deposited in the back of the car and we left Phoebe behind. Phoebe hates the car and is really travel sick, so we felt for the sake of an hour or so we would leave her in the warmth of the kitchen. She stared at us through the windows of the door with eyes like the cat out of Shrek. I closed the front door on her, heart hurting. Phoebe has a soft spot in my heart because of her past. She was rescued from Greece by a magnificently kind lady who makes it her life's work. We really don't know what sort of beginnings Phoebe had but I always feel the human race owes her a debt so I tend to spoil her too much. Phoebe in return cashes in on this big time and has perfected the cat from Shrek look to a tee.

We arrived at the vets and found the door firmly locked. I phoned and this very Welsh lady asked where we were.

'Are you in King Street?'

'I have no idea, I'm in Llanfwr,' I said.

'Where in Llanfwr?' she replied.

'I don't know,' I said weakly.

She had decided by this time she was talking to a complete English idiot and probably isn't far wrong.

'Is the door blue?' she asked.

'Yes!' I replied, relieved we were getting somewhere.

'We haven't been there for three years,' she said, bewildered.

'I only moved here last Wednesday.' I tried to sound intelligent but it wasn't working.

She directed me to the 'new' buildings which Helen and I had passed at least three times and never noticed.

If I say everyone was friendly again I am running the risk of boring you all. So I won't. I will tell you when they are not.

We saw the vet; she duly dipped the wee and Flo did not have diabetes, thank goodness. She did have a urine infection though, and we had her blood taken as he wee showed signs of being alkaline. This was fun. Flo hates anything being interfered with. You can look into any of Phoebe's orifices and she doesn't bat an eyelid… Actually just to be clear we do not look into any of Phoebe's orifices, we just could if we wanted. Flo, on the other hand, will not let you near or by. So four of us backed into a corner of the surgery tried to hold onto her so the vet could take a blood sample. Just shaving her front paw sent Flo into a frenzy. The needle bit was going to be fun! Eventually after pathetic whimpering (that was me and Helen) and many attempts, the sample was taken and we would get the results in an hour.

We were relieved it wasn't diabetes but the vet had mention hyperthyroidism.

Phoebe was fine when we got home and so pleased we hadn't abandoned her in the depths of Wales alone. She needn't have worried; Trevor would have rescued her.

The phone call came and all was normal. To cover the urine infection we are to pick up some antibiotics but the vets feels the rest is the stress of the move, new surroundings, and the fact that her owners are running around like headless chickens. *Phew!*

CHAPTER 5

I have to admit that the novelty of opening boxes has started to wear off a little. The sight of piles of clothes and shoes is grating slightly and not knowing where anything is has gone from an exciting treasure hunt to a phenomenal pain in the arse.

We plod on. After having moved a very large chest of drawers from one room to another we have now decided it is in the wrong place. However, in order for us to get it in the right place we have to saw the legs off. Should be fun. We also have to saw the legs off the wardrobe to be able to get the top on. Fortunately it will not notice but needs must and all that. I just hope Helen doesn't get locked in the wardrobe again during the process.

As we had Flo's antibiotics to pick up and some rawl plugs to get at our friendly builders merchants, this being the nearest thing to a retail fix she is going to get, Helen volunteered to go into Llanfwr. She arrived at the vets at reception and in front of her was a lady chatting away to the receptionist, oblivious to anyone else in the foyer. Helen waited patiently and decided to get the money out ready to pay for Flo's pills. Unfortunately some of the change she had in her purse decided to escape from captivity and make a dash for it, landing at the feet of this woman and beyond.

At this point I should mention that Helen's back, which is always dodgy, is worse at the moment due to all the heavy lifting and shifting we have been doing. She gingerly crouched down on the floor to try and retrieve her coins. The lady was dressed in a tweed skirt and calf-length wellies. After trying to be as inconspicuous as possible she attempted to get up but unfortunately on the way up her head got caught in the woman's skirt and the chatting from above came to an abrupt halt. The woman finally looked down with a bemused look on her face and said with humour, 'Oh, hello!'

Fortunately she saw the funny side of it and they both laughed.

We have managed today to do quite a lot. Some bookcases have been put on walls. Boxes of books unpacked and shelved. Even the Christmas tree has found its way into the living room. It's still in its box but nonetheless the intention to actually put it up is there. Helen has strung some Christmas cards across the beam over the fire which is about as festive as we can manage at the moment.

We have so much to do still but we have only been moved in for just over a week. I'm proud of us. We have worked so hard with barely a cross word and a lot of laughs. This morning a red kite circled overhead looking for prey and glided silently down on some unsuspecting rodent and missed! It soared back over the cottage quite low for a while before decided it was very boring here and flew off. A sight I have longed to see for so long and one that will become commonplace. What an absolute privilege and a joy.

Our very best friends are coming just after Christmas. Carol and Steve. I worked with Carol for years nursing and we have remained firm friends throughout all the trials and tribulations life has piled upon us. Carol and Steve are the friends who are there no matter what. We share so many interests and beliefs, from dogs, animals and politics. We both feel so lucky they are in our lives.

We have ordered the chicken house and run today! Hopefully they will get here before Christmas as my niece Sarah and her husband Robert are also coming for a week in the New Year and if there is anything to be fixed, assembled, tiled or painted then Robert is the man for the job. Sarah is a professional cleaner and whips through the house like a tornado only instead of leaving chaos in its wake she leaves calm and order.

Once Robert has assembled the chicken run we will be getting our three chickens from Trevor in the New Year and will hopefully having fresh eggs daily. I can't wait. We have picked their names, hopefully they will like them; if not we will have to have a sit down discussion but at the end of the day Helen and I will have the final say. It will be essential to establish the pecking order... *Groan.*

Talking of dogs, ours wake us up every morning at roughly seven o'clock. They sleep in our room on their luxury dog bed that I swear would double up as a guest bed. At first we had a few problems orientating them to the new sleeping arrangements; they kept jumping on our bed in the middle of the night resulting in both Helen and I being brought close to cardiac arrest. We worked out that the dogs were getting cold, so now every night we cover them up completely, heads and all, with a blanket and there they stay for the rest of the night until the aforementioned time. It's like having two large furry budgies.

So after this rude awakening we robotically make our way downstairs, and don wellies, hats and coats, put the dogs on their leads and make our way into the blackness of the garden. This morning a crescent moon shone brightly along with the North Star as if to bid us farewell until the next magnificent display. The sky was a Stephens' ink colour, slowly turning into a lighter blue on the horizon, as if the colour had run, like a watercolour wash. As an accompaniment to this visual delight, tawny owls hooted to each other backwards and forwards across our path. An old friend of mine who I only hear from on an ad hoc basis sent me her yearly round-up of events and it ended with, 'So you are in Wales now? Why?' It will be a long reply.

As the upstairs still resembles the back of beyond we concentrated on trying to bring some order to both spare bedrooms. The chest of drawers we shifted from one room yesterday was shifted yet again into our room, as once the bed was up in the guest room there was about a three-inch gap for someone to squeeze through and I don't know anyone who would fit through it; no offence, friends and relatives. It was a worthwhile move though as it looks much better and we can actually walk around the bed.

I carted out boxes, screwed-up paper, looked for things we needed like picture hanging wire; still missing. We put up a bookcase in the guest room. Carried out seven suitcases of clothes (summer) to be stored in the now bursting at the seams garage. Helen worked like a Trojan trying to find room for the few clothes she possesses, not to mention the shoes. They are still homeless to a large extent. My clothes disappeared into one cupboard in a flash. There is a pile of cardboard boxes in the shed that the Welsh Tourist Board have contacted us about as it is threatening to be higher than Mt. Snowdon and may possibly have an adverse effect on the economy of Wales.

We also, in readiness for the grand arrival of our two new sofas, had to get the two recliner chairs we had put in their pro tem from the living room to the conservatory. Recliner chairs are a tad heavy, however, once again the dynamic duo managed it, collapsing into a heap on them once they were in place.

The sofas were due to be delivered between three and six o'clock. They were coming from Swansea and true to form they arrived at five forty-five.

Now I am not an expert in shifting sofas but I could see that these two sofa delivery men were trying to get the sofa in completely the wrong way. We have a small hall and in order to get the sofa in I had already thought that once in the front door, if it was stood on end it would easily go through the living room door. I did suggest it when they first embarked on this but my words fell on deaf ears and a look of, 'We do this all the time, love, you know nothing.' The sofa by this time was stuck in the lounge doorway. They asked me for a Phillips screwdriver and removed the feet and still the sofa would not fit.

'Is there another way into this room?' a muffled voice shouted from behind the sofa.

'Yes,' I replied, 'the back door and lounge double doors behind you.'

'Right,' said the muffled voice. 'Get it back out.'

The sofa was prised out the door and stood on its end in the hallway when suddenly a light bulb went off in both their heads.

'We could get in it on its end!' said one.

'Good idea,' said the other.

I stood and stared then decided to retreat into the kitchen, put my head in my hands and breathe slowly.

The sofa went into the lounge like it had been greased up and fired out of a canon.

CHAPTER 6

Wales is renowned for its overproduction of water from the sky. The grass is squelchy and soggy and the dogs have mud in places I never thought possible. The rain was relentless and in addition to that it was one of those days where we had absolutely nowhere to go and nothing to buy; for a change we thought we would try once again and get the house in order (please note the sarcasm). We had decided that the living room needed attention as the two new sofas were looking down their leather noses at the disarray that surrounded them. First off was to sort the plethora of pictures that were lined up against the wall into what room they would be hung in. Having sort of sorted that, I grabbed my trusty hammer and picture hooks and tried to get a small nail into a three-foot-thick wall. The wall was not playing this game. Out came the drill and I want to personally thank the inventor of the hammer addition as without it I would still be drilling the first hole now.

Pictures were put up, Christmas cards were hung, Helen put up our new Christmas tree and Flo peed on the new rug. Flo never has accidents, today she had two. As she tested negative for diabetes and her bloods were all normal we could only put it down to the urine infection she has, although it was only a slight infection. What puzzles us is that she is clean all night. If it was the infection she would need to pee regardless of the time of day. Personally I think she is stressed. It is all strange to her. Both her mummies are spending most of the day groaning and turning purple and her sister Phoebe is tearing around the garden like something possessed. Talking of which, Helen took them into the garden and was busy in the shed when Flo came into her and led her out the door in time for Helen to see Phoebe's white bum disappearing up the lane toward Trevor's. She shouted for me and by the time I got out there she was in David's garden. Now this all may sound harmless but actually the next turning for her to take would lead her onto a B road or onto a field full of sheep. After much cajoling and offers of two pounds of mature cheddar she wandered back to Helen who rugby tackled her to the floor. Needless to say now she knows how to get out she will not be let off the lead anymore until Freddie the Fencer has done the deed.

However, this did now pose a problem as every trip out means they are both on the lead. To just let Flo off and not Phoebe would be unfair and unmanageable as Pheebs would try to run around the same as Flo.

So the next time they needed to go out and as we were being extra vigilant due to Flo's urinary incontinence, it's become more frequent, I decided to take them out together, lead in each hand. I togged up, wellies, trapper hat, leather gloves and my old but familiar dog-walking coat. Bracing myself before opening the door, I shot out of it and ended up travelling towards the end of the garden like a scene out of the chariot race in Ben-Hur. I have decided next time Helen will accompany me so we can have a bonkers dog each.

My rheumatoid arthritis is playing up, not surprisingly. I am managing to achieve what I want to, but I am propped up by painkillers. Just injected my weekly methotrexate which makes me feel dreadful the day after, so tomorrow will be fun! It didn't help today when I smashed my head on a drainpipe whilst adding more cardboard to Mt. Snowdon the Second. Large lump to top of head but as Helen said, thankfully there is very little to worry about damaging inside my head. Still trying to work out if she meant it or not.

We took delivery of one bathroom cabinet today and get this, a Christmas bouquet of flowers from Mr Removal Manager Man. If he thinks that for all the problems he has caused us and all the breakages we have found, that one pathetic bunch of glitter-covered pine cones and some red roses with tinsel on is going to placate me and the missus, then he either needs a lobotomy or has had one!

I can't believe it's nearly Christmas! What with everything we have had to cope with for the last few weeks Christmas has been the last thing on our minds. We will be on our own but looking forward to it. Following that, our dear friends Carol and Steve are coming to stay and the day they leave my niece Sarah, her son Henry and her husband Robert are visiting for a week, although this will be a mixture of work and pleasure, as Robert is going to retile our bathroom for us and put up a hen house! I can't wait for the girls to join us. Fresh eggs daily; Helen and I will be constipated for weeks.

It was Sunday again, we woke up late for us. Even the dogs snoozed in until eight o'clock. It was raining. I have a feeling there will not be a water ban in the summer but you never know. We dressed in our wet suits and got our snorkels out and walked the dogs.

We are shattered. After yesterday's efforts of drilling through walls, hanging pictures, shifting stuff and generally wearing ourselves out we decided to have a day off. A day of reading papers, listening to the radio and nodding off in front of the log fire, and that's exactly what we did.

We did, however, go into Llanfwr to get some groceries. The choice of shops are either Nisa, Spar or Co-Op. So the Co-Op won. I quite like their Fairtrade policies and the fact that we all get dividends.

We trundled home and after lunch settled onto our new sofas, watched Toy Story (again) and fell asleep. Utter bliss. We have noticed that the less we do the more the dogs are settled and happy. No accidents today from Flo. I read a piece last night on stress symptoms in dogs and Flo displays a fair chunk of them. One of the recommendations was to go stupidly over the top when she pees or poos in the garden and reward her with a treat. This we have duly done all day and I am sure now both dogs are squeezing one out to get at the dog treats we carry around in our coat pockets. One of our old dogs, Dorcas, used to pretend to pee. She would squat as if she was going but nothing came out.

Sunday was always one of the days I visited my mum and sometimes I forget she is not there anymore and a sudden panic sweeps over me that haven't seen her, and then I remember. I am pragmatic most of the time and say all the platitudes to myself like, 'she was ninety-eight,' and, 'she had a good life,' but at the end of the day, she was my mum and you only get the one, and because she lived to such an age you actually think they will always be there and go on forever. It actually came as a shock when it happened. So much has occurred in the time surrounding her fall, illness and death, I feel like I haven't given myself any time to just grieve. No doubt it will come.

We saw Trevor when we were in our garden and he told us that his wife Jill's mother died the night before. It was sort of expected but as we know only too well, you are never prepared.

We went over with a Christmas card and some wine with also a sympathy card. She is lovely, Jill, a down-to-earth lady. They have a lovely home and we stayed and had coffee and chatted. They are coming over for an evening meal in the New Year. I think we are going to have firm friends there. Trevor was his usual self but you could see how caring he was to his wife and so supportive. A lovely couple. He did though, in true Trevor fashion, offer to prepare the pheasants in the garden should Phoebe eventually get one. 'They are great in a stir fry,' he said to Helen. The look on her face was priceless, a cross between trying to look grateful whilst secretly being horrified.

Today feeling better. I had most of the day to myself as Helen had to go into Carmarthen to attend the bank for an appointment. So I set about clearing some of the stuff that was propped against walls and not doing anything. I also took arrival of our new bathroom tiles and our chicken hut! Really, really cannot wait for that to be in place and the girls to come. Names to follow.

I tidied the utility room and found things I never knew we had and also things I wondered why we had them. I even found the floor.

The living room is now almost clear apart from the 200 or so books we haven't got a home for. I was going to say maybe we have too many books but you can never have too many books.

Plastic boxes were put into the shed; the removal company was called to pick up the millions of flattened cardboard boxes. I ordered the Calor gas for the range cooker and generally felt I had been quite industrious.

It was odd being in this house without Helen, who was fighting her way through the Christmas crowds in Carmarthen. She witnessed a fight between two men, she thinks in their sixties, in the Marks and Spencer car park. They were shouting at each other evidently, one in his car and the other was pushing his body on the driver's door to prevent the driver getting out. It didn't work and out of this tiny Fiat got the most enormous man who shoved the other man so hard he ended up a few feet away on his behind! So a cultured introduction to Carmarthen was experienced.

The weather is dull, foggy, wet without rain, so damp in other words. Even the birds look depressed. We feed them daily and can hear them chattering amongst themselves as we fill up their feeders and replenish the water and fat ball holders. It's almost as if they are saying, 'There she is, great, fresh food, pass it on.' There is evidence of foxes in the garden so that will be a concern when the chickens arrive. Evidently according to Trevor, rats eat chickens too. I love nature and wildlife but the human in me does find it brutal at times, however, at least everything they do is for survival, unlike us who kill for fun, sport or sheer greed.

Helen came home with some Christmas food. She got her turkey crown, some more mince pies and one more shop and we should be sorted. We are looking forward to our Christmas, just us and the dogs. Ah, the dogs, therein lies a tail… Ouch, pun!

The dogs are still jumping on our bed in the middle of the night; evidently Helen still thinks it is because they are cold. They have been covered up as said before with a fleece blanket. So tonight, the plan is to give them a quilt all of their own. Call me a sceptic but I think it's that they need the pack all together. However, after a particularly pungent aroma hitting the air in the middle of the night we both decided Flo's anal glands were on the rampage. Consequently the first chore of the morning consisted of me watching a YouTube video on how to find and squeeze a dog's anal glands. Who says I don't have fun? Having watched this enchanting video, I set about to emulate the procedure. Flo wasn't impressed. Armed with rubber gloves, Vaseline and kitchen roll I successfully emptied said glands while Helen held Flo's head and retched. We make a good team.

We do not have normal days here. Even though we are living in a community of about twelve people at most, our door knocker is busy.

Gwen the postwoman, in addition to bringing our post and parcels, comes in and feeds the dogs a treat every day. Flo and Phoebe fully expect it now. I caught Flo looking at the clock today as Gwen was late. So she was our first visitor.

After feeding the birds and getting in the logs, the Calor gas man arrived and showed me how to connect and switch the bottles to fire up the range.

I got on with the usual housework chores and Helen decided on putting her clothes away. If anyone reading this has seen Helen's clothes collection then they know this is no easy feat. Whilst doing this she happened to look out of the window to see one of Owain's dogs, Lily, heading down the lane. Flo and Phoebe had clocked her too and were by now beside themselves barking to ensure Lily didn't come anywhere near their house. Trevor togged up and lead in hand made towards the dog. I kept an eye out to see how this all progressed and after about ten minutes I saw Lily in the lane but no Helen. So I put on my wellies and coat, grabbed another lead and headed off in the same direction only to find Helen and Trevor chin-wagging at the end of the lane surrounded by Owain's four dogs. It transpires Lily was just off the lead out for a walk in one of the surrounding fields and not out alone at all! We all ended up chatting for ages, ignoring the fact that fine rain was actually soaking all of us.

This is a special announcement! Alert the media! Helen has hung all her clothes in wardrobes and wall cupboards! The clothes rail that was in the other house is no more. It is dismantled and in the garage. I cannot tell you how thrilled I am that I do not have to look at it anymore. We were making headway and by five o'clock the spare rooms were habitable. They look like bedrooms, the Tetris room is no more.

Halfway through this Mary, David's wife, came over with a Christmas present and card. She is an Irish lady with a wonderful Southern Irish lilt to her voice and a twinkle in her eye. I should imagine she would be a very entertaining dinner guest and has a few stories to tell. We chatted away for ages easily as if we had known each other years. In the New Year we are all getting together here, Trevor and Jill, Mary and David, and we are very much looking forward to that. I have a feeling it is going to be riotous. We took in a parcel for David this morning and when we gave it to Mary to give to him, she said, 'Oh, it's probably a brain or something. I'll stick it in the fridge.' Bearing in mind David is a forensic pathologist we were not entirely convinced she was joking.

Just as we were winding down and about to feed the dogs and start our own dinner there was yet another knock on the door. It was Trevor and Jill just popping in to see if we were OK and as Trevor said, 'Get the kettle on,' I duly did and they stayed for about an hour. They gave us huge insight into the sleepy hamlet we have joined and it appears in the past it's had its moments regarding past occupants. I think the collective get-together is going to be very revealing and a hoot!

So here we are finally fed and relaxing. Although Helen is still looking for somewhere to shelve the books. I have a feeling another bookcase purchase is on the cards.

The dogs persist in their nightly sneaking onto our bed in the night and we are so shattered we either can't be bothered to rouse ourselves to get them on their own bed or are so fast asleep we don't feel them get up. Either way, they get to sleep on our bed and most of the time on us! The result is both Helen and I, because of the positions we end up in to avoid the dogs, not being able to actually stand up straight when we get out of bed. So, walking like Quasimodo with gout we make our way downstairs to the back door to put wellies on and coats over our nightwear. Fabulous look. Thank goodness no-one can see us. Actually it's so dark we can't even see us.

As we made such good headway yesterday we felt we earned a trip out to Llanfwr as we had found an antiques centre there that we hadn't explored to date. The usual drive took us through the hillsides full of sheep and low-lying cloud that clung to the side of the higher hills as if it was scared to let go and disappear into oblivion. We arrived at the antiques centre. It's one of those warehouse-type centres where at each turn there is a different unit with various items. We walked through past the glass cabinets full of old china and jewellery, stopping every now and again to read the descriptions of certain items and the history behind them. Off to one side was a little room full of antique rugs. We have a thing for old rugs and have a few already but there was this one rug, deep red with a subtle pattern and perfect for our landing. The whole of the upstairs is oak flooring so rugs are perfect for it. I managed to knock twenty-five pounds off the price and we walked away happy as a pig in poo.

Right next to the antique centre wedged in-between that and the garden centre is a little café called 'Two Soups'. It is named after the sketch written by one of our comedy heroines Victoria Wood. If you have never seen it with Julie Waters playing the main part, YouTube it. It is sheer comedic genius. We ventured in and it was like stepping back in time. In the corner was an old gramophone and although hooked up to a iPod playing 1930s music it seemed authentic. There is only room for about sixteen people to be seated at one time but it was cosy and friendly. We ordered tea and toasted sandwiches and whilst we were waiting one couple, obviously regulars, got up to leave. The conversation went like this:

Man to owner: 'So are you ready for Christmas then?'

Owner: 'No, I hate it. Every bit of it.'

Man, in a surprised voice: 'Why is that then?'

Owner: 'Probably because I am a miserable cow, it just means you have to be nice for the day to people you don't particularly like and why? Everyone is under so much pressure to be joyful and actually no-one really is, we are all just pretending. I'm spending it with my daughter and it's always a disaster.'

Man (obviously hesitant as to what to say next): 'Well I hope you enjoy being miserable then.'

Laughter followed this remark and he looked at me.

'I bet you wished you never asked,' I said with a smile.

Nodding and donning his coat and hat, he and his wife left.

The owner came over to us with our food and apologised for being so negative but she was smiling and I felt that most of the conversation was said mostly as banter.

We thoroughly enjoyed the atmosphere of the place and know it is going to be 'our place' where we go and have a cup of tea and lunch occasionally.

After this we went around the town; the pavements are so narrow you walk along a little bit like you are on a tightrope. Today being the shortest day of the year we found partly due to the dullness of the weather and partly because of the daylight hours that by two thirty in the afternoon shop lights were going on and cars were putting on their headlights.

We made our way home happy and content as usual. The rug looks wonderful and we have added a few more homely touches to the upstairs and the house is really looking like home now, which of course it is.

The next day dawned and what a day it turned out to be!

It all started much the same as any other day and we were dragging our heels as normal, ambling about in PJs and wellies as you do, when Freddie the Fencer turned up a day early. We of course were pleased as punch. It means the dogs will not have to go out in the garden on a lead and can run off all their excess energy and possibly stop getting on our bed. We can but hope.

Freddie had also bought a trailer load of logs so he set about loading them into our wood shed for us, taking out the existing logs and putting the new logs to the back. He did this and then said he would be right back as he needed to go to the builders' merchants to get some more staples.

Just as he left my phone rang and it was the Swansea removal branch ringing to say they were going to collect the mountain of cardboard cartons and boxes that were lurking in the shed. So off we went to the shed and started to chuck the flattened boxes out to stack in the drive. There were hundreds of them and we also started to try and empty some that were filled with tools and pictures etc. so they would not be left behind. The men arrived and started loading the van. It was a huge relief to us to see them gone. The shed resembles a shed now and not a recycling centre. I also found my sunglasses... not that I need them.

Just as the removal men left Freddie turned up again and another van arrived behind him. This was a Christmas delivery of my methotrexate injections... Oh, joy.

Freddie set about starting on the fence and checked the perimeter to ensure all possible escape routes for Phoebe were foiled. I made him a cup of tea and in the meantime Helen decided to go to Lampeter Sainsbury's to get the rest of the grocery shopping in. I stayed behind to ensure Freddie didn't dehydrate or die of hunger.

I went out into the garden to feed the birds as usual and was halfway through this when I heard Trevor shouting, 'Oi!' He had been and had a haircut and I remarked on how dashing he was looking to which he told me to stop taking the proverbial. He handed me a bag of lamb chops for Helen and told me he would be giving me a leg of lamb 'for my people when they come after Christmas'. I thanked him and we stood and chatted for ages. Trevor can talk and then talk some more and then just in case that's not enough he talks a little bit further.

I made my way back indoors after having finished the birds but not before I chatted to Freddie for about a quarter of an hour or so.

I managed to clean some of the house and we have found a solution to the book problem. The stairs! Just a few on one side actually looks quite Bohemian so for now part of the library can be read whilst ascending the stairs. The rest of the books have been piled up by the side of the bookcase, neatly of course. I did realise as I was randomly picking books and stacking them that Helen would have the equivalent of a cerebral thrombosis when she saw how random the books actually were. Helen likes to put all the wildlife books together, gardening, authors, etc., etc. Get the picture? I have just chucked them willy-nilly on the stairs and bookcase. She is too knackered to notice yet but I am quite confident once she notices it will keep her awake until all is back into her ordered, alphabetised regime.

I was just thinking about making a cup of tea when there was a knock on the door. It was Trevor with Thomas, his little boy. After introducing myself to Thomas, aged five, I asked him if he had been a good boy for Father Christmas and his daddy. Thomas looked at me, nodded his head uncertainly and announced he felt he had been, 'Good enough.' The reason for the second encounter with Trevor was he had brought breast of lamb for our dogs. So I gathered some celebration sweets and put them into a bag and gave them to Thomas and in the meantime Trevor and Freddie had started chatting but as I could barely understand a word they were saying because of their very strong Welsh accents, I made my excuses and went back indoors. Half an hour later Helen arrived back from Lampeter and evidently her sat nav had taken her through fields and up mountains and nearly through someone's kitchen.. The car, Helen's pride and joy, was filthy. We all chatted for another ten or so minutes as the two men were still nattering. Having got in the shopping, made a cup of tea and finished the housework, I looked out and guess what? The men were still talking! In all they talked for two hours. I was getting ready to put them up over Christmas and lay two more places for the dinner table when I saw Trevor and Thomas disappear up the lane.

Freddie continued the fencing and finally he was finished. Once he had gone we let the dogs run to their hearts' delight. By the time they finished they were asking to come in. Phoebe was still looking to see if there was a way she could run for the hills but it was Phoebe-proof.

Helen had purchased sausages in the Llanfwr butchers yesterday on recommendation from Trevor and Jill and I promised I would cook them for her tonight. I had just started the evening meal when the knocker went on the front door. There stood two women and a girl. They introduced themselves as the neighbours who live in another cottage on the estate. They were mother and daughter and granddaughter. They had brought us a Christmas gift to welcome us and gave us their phone numbers and invited us in the New Year to come over for a drink and a 'get to know you' evening.

I have never in all the places I have lived known such generosity of spirit. It restores my faith in human nature.

The welcome to Wales has been amazing. The countryside is amazing. The people are amazing. Happy? Never been happier.

CHAPTER 7

The dogs are enjoying their newfound freedom although Flo has also found the compost heap. It appears that the previous owners had put what looked like some sort of fat on the heap, I'm guessing from a BBQ, and in amongst this enormous pile of rotting vegetation Flo uncovers it and eats a substantial amount. Helen reckons it may well shoot out of her later. Phoebe on the other hand was tucking into the birds' mealworms as I had left the lid off the container. We do feed these dogs, honestly.

I ended up trying to fence off the bits of the compost heap that Flo could gain access into with some plastic mesh and metal stakes. Feeling quite accomplished at the end of this I trudged back into the house only to look out of the kitchen window to see Flo's head bobbing up and down over the compost fencing, eating to her heart's delight whatever it was. There are now some plastic chairs strategically placed to try and stop Flo's garden banqueting.

We finished our Christmas food shopping and tried out Nisa, an independent local supermarket, nationally known but selling local stuff. It was OK but we were not spoilt for choice. We ended up in the Co-Op. Petrol got for the car and more kindling, we set off on the sleepy drive back home. I must have counted at least half a dozen red kites soaring overhead terrorising everything under them and other birds in their path. They are magnificent to see. The pure red bodies and the contrasting white on their wings are such a welcome sight on these grey, damp, drab, sombre days of midwinter. There were a few buzzards also and again these are wonderful on the eye. There is nowhere around here that doesn't really please the vision. Even our little town is full of charm. It was busy today by comparison to other days. Last-minute Christmas shoppers trying to at least manage Christmas Eve as a day of rest.

Popped in on the way home to see Gareth, our friendly builders' merchant, and bought some coat hooks for the back of the bathroom door to hang towels on.

We got home and titivated the rooms. Hanging mirrors and removing boxes. Making up spare beds and changing ours. The main guest room is lovely now and the views from the windows will be a delight to look at on waking. I quite envy our guests.

The dogs settled and so did we after our evening meal. Helen has found the air vent on the log burner and so the mystery of the dying flames has been solved. Well done, M. The TV programming was putrid. We ended up with Crocodile Dundee on of all things! Talk about dated and banal. I decided to colour my hair and shave my legs and actually do something nice for myself to make me feel a female human being again. The hair has turned out well, the legs are bald, now if I can just find those tweezers, the purple ones with the spots on, I can attack my Chewbacca eyebrows and I will be a happy girl.

I love Christmas Eve, I prefer it to Christmas Day. Christmas Eve is full of expectation of what will be. The presents, the family get-togethers, the TV programmes, crackers, peanuts and roast dinners and Brussel's sprouts that went on in November.

I always think of all the children out there who still believe in Father Christmas and want to go to bed at three o'clock in the afternoon. The reason I prefer it is, in reality, Christmas Day rarely lives up to the vision we had. The roast dinner is late (my mum used to say it's because everyone is using the gas or electric so it's slowed down), the kids have broken their new toys or you forgot to get batteries or you got the wrong ones. The TV turns out to be rubbish and you cook too many Brussel's or get wind from them and spend the day very uncomfortably sitting on one cheek and no-one has room for the Christmas pudding, swearing they will have it later and never do.

Helen and I decided we have got two days off. Two days off from unpacking, tidying, moving furniture etc. We have made such good progress we feel we can just sit back on our laurels and just be. So we set about just pottering; no pictures went up, no drill was used and not one nail was hammered.

I was just about to make some tea late morning when a familiar strong Welsh accent drifted in from the conservatory. Angel Trevor had turned up to invite us over tonight for drinks and food. We willingly accepted and he sat and had a coffee then went on his way.

The afternoon was spent doing nothing, pure bliss. The weather is atrocious. Wind and rain, but the cottage as it turns out is lovely and warm.

We got ourselves ready, not knowing really how to dress, so we went for casual but smart and made our way over to Trevor and Jill's clutching bottles. Trevor opened the door wearing a rainbow-coloured knitted jumper, Spider-Man pyjama bottoms, slippers made to look like foxes with long tails that dangled proudly at the back, and a nightcap-type hat in equally vibrant colours. This man is completely bonkers.

The welcome we got and the food we were served was beautiful. Helen at one point was literally crying with laughter at Trevor's stories. Suffice to say we had a riot of a time. I sat there thinking we have known these people three weeks, if that, and already they feel like old friends. Jill plays straight man to Trevor's comedic genius to perfection. They obviously adore each other. We left at midnight. Evidently Helen and Trevor are going fly fishing at some point in the New Year and Jill and I are going to sit in a dinghy ensuring they don't get too drunk and drown. They are also going to the pub in Llanffas and I am the designated driver for the evening and goodness knows what else. Helen and Trevor together are so funny and it was brilliant to see her so happy. After all we have endured, to find this piece of paradise doesn't make any of it worthwhile but it certainly dulls the pain at times.

Poor Jill has only just lost her mum and it would have been her mother's birthday yesterday. We also had an insight into Trevor's very humble beginnings and how this pure, kind soul survived that and became this beautiful human being is testament to what the human spirit can endure, survive and achieve.

CHAPTER 8

Last year there were thirteen people for Christmas dinner at ours. All the family were together and I am so glad that I got my mum home to enjoy what turned out to be her last Christmas with her family. I can't stress enough how important it is to make these memories, to be nice to each other and above all know that in a blink of an eye it can all change, so we should make the most of every minute.

So this Christmas was a day of reflection for both of us. Helen and I spoke about how hard days like Christmas Day are for those of us who feel incomplete. Nothing will ever heal the gaps that are left in our lives when someone we love so dearly dies. We just have to learn to live with these enormous great emotional holes that we are left with. Some days will always be better than others but on emotive days like yesterday, anniversaries of every kind or just even when a song or certain words are uttered we find ourselves plunged into another time or place momentarily and it is a heart wrenching, overwhelming moment in an otherwise OK day.

The weather was atrocious. As we live in a valley the wind can get (we are informed by you know who) up to sixty miles an hour. And he is not wrong; take it from me ,the wind is strong. So after letting the dogs out yesterday they came back into our conservatory covered in mud and I mean covered. We decided after that to take them out on leads to cut down on the time it took us to clean them up and the washing of wet, muddy dog towels. I have one of those fur-lined trapper hats, especially bought to make me look like a mad old post-menopausal woman and also to walk the dogs in inclement weather. It has a clip underneath the chin to ensure it doesn't fly off in high winds. It doesn't work. A gust of wind caught it just right resulting in air inflating the hat to make me look like my skull had expanded six inches on top and the strap securing it underneath nearly strangled me. This coupled with the wind and rain and being pulled around the garden by Phoebe in search of terrorising pheasants did not make for a pleasant, leisurely dog walk.

We opened our presents and both of us were delighted with the results. Helen had got me all the things I wanted and hopefully vice versa. Especially pleased with my Hilary Clinton *What Happened* book and Roy Orbison CD. I love Roy. I never really did when he was in the charts back in the day but as I have got older I have appreciated his music and the joy it brings. We do change as the years advance in our taste, well at least I have. We actually put on Top of the Pops yesterday whilst opening our presents and both remarked on how every song sounded like the last. On reflection this is without doubt exactly the same words our parents were tutting and rolling eyes to back in the 1960s and 70s when we thought our music was the best.

Our Christmas dinner was lovely and despite the fact that Helen had a hangover from her evening with Trevor she did her best to soldier on through, although the copious amounts of vitamin C drinks and glasses of water indicated to me she was slightly if not totally dehydrated. Bless.

Just a lazy day although Flo has developed a dislike for the TV. We had on a nature programme and this baby penguin was on the screen looking for its mum. Flo clocked it and went berserk! We were so scared she would just jump up at the TV and knock it over we had to restrain her, hanging onto her collar while she growled at the screen. Naturally we thought this was because it was another animal but lo and behold she then progressed onto barking at the news, Carols from Kings and Toy Story. Why she has suddenly started this is a mystery. It's all rather disturbing, one minute you are watching Buzz Lightyear save the day and the next Flo suddenly lets rip this ear-piercing bark right in your lughole! Talk about jump! The resultant mayhem of us both yelling at her through our palpitations and then wrestling her to the floor to grab her collar and pull her away from knocking the TV flying certainly disrupts the peace and quiet of our abode.

I spoke to two of my 'kids'. My poor daughter had worked a twelve-hour shift in the nursing home and was doing exactly the same Boxing Day. She is spending two weeks here soon so I shall spoil her then, and my eldest son was celebrating not only Christmas but his partner's birthday. My youngest son is in Sri Lanka with his family in shorts and tee shirts and in some ways I do envy them, especially when I am taking the dogs out.

Boxing Day is always a relief. The pressure is off, the dinner is easy. Well, ours always is – cold meats, buttery mash, peas and whatever sauces, pickles etc. that take your fancy. I prefer this dinner to a roast, don't ask me why. Simple, I guess.

We spent the Boxing Day pottering. As our dear friends Carol and Steve arrive tomorrow as our first house guests we wanted to make the house look as nice as possible. At the end of the afternoon we started a game of Monopoly which we abandoned after two long hours on the excuse that we needed to start dinner but actually we were both bored beyond comprehension. I have to say I was winning, I had all the yellows, all the greens, the blues and the stations in-between, that corner of the board was mine, all mine.

So the next day, the big day had arrived and we were so excited about seeing Carol and Steve again. Carol and I nursed together for many years and have become very close. They are the type of friends who would drop anything they were doing and put you first if you needed them. Friends like these are precious.

When we viewed the house back in September the previous owners had a beautiful wooden plate rack on the kitchen wall. We enquired as to whether they would sell it with the house but they explained it was a gift and they didn't want to part with it. Knowing Steve was brilliant at carpentry I asked him if he could make one identical based on one photo. From this he used the tiles underneath the rack in the photo as a guide to size and counted the gaps in the plate rails to establish the width. He brought it today along with a barn owl box and a tawny owl box for our garden. They are all amazing, but the plate rack is superb. It is even better than the one we wanted. He also announced they were our housewarming gift. We both cried. We have been deeply touched by the kindness of strangers in the past three weeks and now completely bowled over by this gesture of friendship. We are so lucky.

We all enjoyed a lovely leisurely lunch and have not stopped talking and laughing all day and evening. They love Ty Mawr and I know and also pray they will be regular visitors.

Flo loves Steve. It is intense. You can feel the attraction she feels for him as soon as he walks in the room. The demonstration of her fervour takes the form of trying to sit on him at every given opportunity, wrapping herself around his shoulders like a fur stole and drooling like there is no tomorrow. She is a shameless hussy and she doesn't care.

The weather today has been varied to say the least. This morning we awoke to bright sunshine, wet underfoot from yesterday's deluge but almost warm. By the time Carol and Steve arrived the sky was overcast and sleep and rain descended. Within minutes it was sunny again and then the temperature dropped dramatically and tonight on our last outing with the dogs we crunched the frost underneath our feet on the grass. I would not be at all surprised if we wake up to some snow. The air has that feel about it. I have always noticed a certain type of smell in the air and a stillness as if the whole of the environment is waiting in anticipation for the blanket of white ice to fall and encompass it in its freezing embrace. Then again I could be wrong.

So I sit here in bed typing away surrounded by two snoring dogs and one very exhausted snoring Helen. Hopefully I shall be a snoring Hannah soon but I guarantee the moment I switch everything off and lie down I will be wide awake.

C'est la vie.

CHAPTER 9

As mentioned before, our amazing friends Carol and Steve visited for a few days and it was lovely. Steve put together the chicken house and run, minus the wire netting as he ran out of time. He sorted out the wardrobe in the bedroom and made it fit! And all this time Carol, Helen and I helped where we could and spent the rest of the time catching up. It was a lovely visit.

The day they left, my niece Sarah and her husband Robert came along with Harry my great-nephew. We had decided to make New Year special and all had stockings full of presents to open, table presents, and a New Year's dinner. We played games in the evening and we all enjoyed ourselves, it was like a second Christmas Day.

The next day Robert set about retiling our upstairs bathroom and so spent the week making a superb job of it. We are really pleased with the end result, new cabinet, new towel rail and the tiles are lovely. So that's the first room done to our taste. It's been a lovely week with lots of laughs, a few tears remembering my mum and of course Sarah's nan.

The wire was also put on the chicken run and two days later Trevor and Jill were standing at our front door, Trevor with a chicken under his arm and Jill with two in a cat carrier; luckily for the chickens the cat wasn't in it. They are beautiful. We have named them Edna, Gladys and Gertie (EGG). It hasn't been plain sailing.

The run is brilliant, as is the hen house. We kept them in for the first twenty-four hours as instructed then let them out to enjoy the grounds and get used to their new abode. Sarah and I decided to go into Llanfwr for some shopping and lunch and left Robert busy in the bathroom and Helen busy with the house, dogs and chooks… and that's where it all went horribly wrong.

Evidently while we were out and the chickens were scratching their way around their new estate, surveying the view, Helen in her infinite wisdom decided to see how the dogs and the chickens embraced each other and bonded. They didn't.

The dogs made a beeline for the run, barking and manically jumping up the coop. Flo was chewing at the wire, the hens were going berserk and flying up in the air, feathers everywhere. Trevor heard the commotion and came running down the lane as he thought a fox must have got in the pen and between them armed with sticks (not to hit them with I must add) they managed to get the dogs back in the house and survey the damage on the chickens. Fortunately, apart from ruffled feathers they were OK but traumatised. They had to be locked up in their house to calm them down. When Sarah and I got home Helen looked like she had been dragged around the garden, through the shrubbery and had a bucket of mud thrown over her.

So we now have a dilemma. We can't let the dogs out when the chickens are out unless the dogs are on a lead. We are walking them the other side of the garden for the time being but Helen has a cunning plan and it involves the dovecote, AKA hencote. The plan is to move the whole run and hen house so the house is in the actual dovecote and the run attached to the door of it so they have complete safety at night as we can shut the door and we can fence that side of the garden off so the dogs can't get to the hens. I think this will all happen at some point next week, but it's going to have to be soon. Needless to say, the donkey, sheep, goats and anything else we flippantly said we would like won't be happening even if it ever was! We will, however, be definitely keeping bees and look forward to their arrival.

The weather is atrocious. I know the rest of the country has taken a battering too. It is wet, muddy and windy. I have given up trying to keep the conservatory floor clean although I am having a breakdown every time I have to look at it. We have washable mats by the door which are sodden with mud and are washed and changed on a regular basis but you wouldn't know it to look at them.

The lounge has curtains! The beautiful old arched windows in there look even better now they are draped in an understated floral design that Carol and I picked when she was here. Sarah and I put them up and I have to say I am chuffed to bits with the overall effect.

On another note, evidently my snoring has become a problem. According to Helen it has reached the same noise level as a rock concert or a volcanic eruption. I do suffer with sinusitis on a regular basis so that could be one of the reasons for this sudden regurgitation of a past problem that I thought had resolved itself. Another is that I am sleeping on my back due to sciatica which is worse whatever side I lie on. Consequently, Helen hates me every morning. The spare room has beckoned more than once and it appears to be the only solution at present; it's either that or she will kill me, painfully. If the blog stops without explanation ring the police please.

I got up earlier than Helen as she had slipped into a sleep-deprived coma and took the dogs out, let the chickens out and made the tea. Sarah and Robert were leaving this morning after breakfast and they started to get themselves ready for their journey home. After we were all up and I fed the dogs and Helen and I took them out on their leads for a post-prandial poo. We were ambling around the garden when Phoebe launched into a barking fit and we realised Trevor, Jill, Thomas and four dogs were standing at our fence. We were invited to join them on their morning dog walk but aware that Sarah and Robert were departing soon I declined, but Helen happily joined them. Thomas calls her Helens and grabbed her hand as they all walked off down the lane.

Sarah and Robert were almost ready to leave and we had a last cup of tea before their journey and killed some time waiting for the return of Helen and the dogs. It didn't happen. After forty or so minutes the general consensus was that they had either a) walked a long way, b) one of the dogs was lost (I was guessing Phoebe) or c) they had all fallen into the river. I was partially right on two counts. After waving off Sarah and Robert I pottered about indoors. Then inspected the hens and generally made myself useful. I did start to worry slightly after the first hour had passed, then slightly more after a further thirty minutes had elapsed when eventually Helen arrived red-faced and worn out. The dogs were covered in mud and looked ready to drop. Phoebe as I suspected had decided to push the boundaries of tolerance and as the surrounding area is full of pheasants she had obviously caught the scent of something and had disappeared into the ether pro tem. Helen was obviously concerned but Trevor decided the best tactic was to walk in the opposite direction and she would come back. Well, it did work but not until about half an hour later. Goodness only knows what she had been up to but she was extremely wet and muddy on her return.

After cleaning up the dogs and having a cup of tea we decided to go into Llanfwr for some food bits and pieces and Helen wanted to show me the pet food warehouse en route (who says romance is dead?) What amazed me more than anything is I got quite excited at the thought... What has happened to me? So after dragging ourselves around the Co-Op we set off to the pet warehouse via Helen's inbuilt satellite navigation system which consisted of her remembering where it is after Trevor took her about a week ago. We got lost. When we eventually arrived at our destination on an industrial estate that had heavy grey metal fencing and gates everywhere giving the impression of an internment camp, it was shut. So we turned around and made our way home. After getting lost again and ending up where we started we had both grown tired of the never-ending winding roads of the Welsh countryside with magnificent views and were gagging for a drink but most of all a pee! I think my urethral sphincter has had the work out of its life!

So that was our day really. The sun shone, the rain didn't happen and the cold froze the marrow in your bones, however, after an evening meal and a log fire burning away, TV on watching rubbish, we both feel human again. We are all very relaxed and happy. What more could you want?

CHAPTER 10

Fearing a slow, painful death at the hands of Helen should the snoring continue, I decided that I would try to sleep on my side which I did albeit uncomfortably at first. But, being the stoic, strong, non-complaining creature I am, I persevered and drifted off into a dreamless sleep, safe in the knowledge that I wouldn't be stabbed at any point in the night. I wasn't stabbed, but in the early hours of the morning I suddenly felt this very cold, wet fluid soaking the right side of my arm and face. Helen had woken up thirsty. She keeps a pint glass of water on her bedside cabinet to satiate any nightly dehydration. Last night she decided she would attempt to be the only person in the world who could drink lying flat on their back. Slowly reaching for the full glass she manoeuvred it over her chest in line with her gob and tipped the lot over herself, me and the bedding. To say it was a rude awakening would be understating what it feels like to suddenly find your warm bed is covered in ice-cold water. We both shot out of the waterlogged bed as she explained what had happened. The bed was soaked. The bottom sheet, the mattress protector (Helen is worried I may suddenly become incontinent), the pillows and the duvet cover not to mention our night clothes. Stripping off both ourselves and the bed I suddenly became aware that the little window in our bedroom overlooked the garden and if Trevor had happened to be in the wrong place at the wrong time he would be treated to the sight of Helen and myself in all our glory running around our bed flinging sheets and duvets around. He may have thought it was some strange same sex ritual. I am really hoping he was asleep.

So after that commotion I did manage to go back to sleep but unfortunately snored, however, given the kerfuffle caused by Helen she did not complain.

I'm slow to get started in the mornings courtesy of my rheumatoid arthritis and when Helen announced we were going to move the hens into the dovecote and their run etc., I inwardly groaned, knowing that this wasn't going to be a walk in the park. Regardless of my fears we dressed accordingly and launched ourselves into the foray! The first task was to dog-proof the side of the garden the dovecote is on. This is on the far side of the stream so both bridges had to be inaccessible to them. We found an old gate in the dovecote for one of them and I put up some wire netting on the other. Pleased so far with our efforts we congratulated ourselves on being brilliant and then we looked at the hen coop and house and realised it wasn't going to happen, not with just us two anyway. We came to the conclusion after about ten minutes, that standing in the middle of the garden looking at each other gormlessly wasn't going to produce any brainwaves on how to tackle this problem, until a very small lightbulb went on in my brain and I decided to phone Trevor... Who else?

Jill answered the phone and I explained our dilemma. At this Trevor shouted he was on his way and Jill said he had never been so relieved to hear the phone ring as she was going through old family photos with him.

He arrived and so did Jill ready and willing to shift the coop and lend a hand. After having got the hens into Phoebe's dog crate we decided the best way to shift the coop was for all four of us to grab a corner and carry it up the lane and over the fence. We all took our places, Trevor at the back on my side and Jill and Helen manning the other. Now Trevor is a big chap, strong and also has no idea how strong, so consequently he was charging forward at a much quicker pace than my legs could carry me. He also wasn't watching how I was doing and what direction he was hurtling me in. It was a conifer tree and even when I had become completely engulfed in it, pinned between the trunk and the chicken coop, the penny still hadn't dropped. Fortunately Jill and Helen saw my legs hanging out of the tree and heard my frantic cries of, 'Stop!' When they eventually could speak due to hysterical laughter they shouted for Trevor to cease his onslaught. I extracted myself with as much dignity I could muster in a trapper hat with twigs and branches stuck in various places and we proceeded up the lane. We got the run in place and secured it to the dovecote and Trevor and I went off to get the hen house while Helen and Jill dug a little trench to level the coop out. The idea was to get the hen house into the dovecote so at night they can be locked in safely away from any predators of which around here there are many. Once we were finished we all trundled inside for a well-deserved cup of tea and slice of Steve's amazing ginger cake. We remarked that ginger cake was appropriate for Trevor as he is a redhead but he prefers to call his hair colour 'African Sunset'.

Once they had gone home, Helen and I added all the finishing touches and as the sun was going down we put the girls to bed and I could hear Helen saying to them, 'Night-night, girls, sleep tight, see you in the morning.'

Edna, Gladys and Gertie are actually in much better shape than we are. We didn't even have the energy to cook dinner and barely enough to eat it, so we ended up with cheese and crackers.

Now sitting here by the log fire, showered and stiff and sore from head to toe. Each time one of us gets up to attempt to move we perform an uncanny impersonation of a cross between Quasimodo and an ageing sloth.

I don't care if I do snore tonight, I could not care less. I have a feeling we will both be in a coma anyway.

So the next day we decided we needed logs for the wood burner and the last small amount we bought were very damp and not worth paying out for again. Consequently we bought a large amount of kiln-dried logs and they were to be delivered this afternoon.

Our plan was to return to the romantic destination of the pet food warehouse in Llanefwr to treat the chickens to mixed corn. This is a treat as usually the pellets suffice but in this cold weather they need extra food so feeding them mixed corn in the afternoon helps them at night time as it is slow to digest, therefore causing inner central heating for chooks! We also needed dog food, hay etc. However, that was before Trevor brought round some freshly laid eggs from his older birds and stayed for coffee. We get up fairly early but by the time we have fed the dogs, let the chickens out and fed them, run the dogs and had breakfast and showered it's mid-morning. Walking the dogs and feeding chickens still in your pyjamas is normal here, evidently. Well it is now, anyway.

Trevor departed and we awaited the logs. They arrived in a tip-up truck. Fortunately Trevor had told us to put tarpaulin down on our drive as when the logs get tipped all sorts gets tipped with them. It took about two minutes to dump hundreds of logs on our drive and an hour and a half to put them all in the woodshed. Clearing up the tarpaulin Helen found an enormous tooth! An 'eye' tooth or canine tooth to give it its proper name. We think it's from a pig but could be anything really as we are not experts on teeth! It is about two inches long so whatever it belonged to could have taken a fair chunk out of whatever it wanted to. Anyway, we were knackered by the time we had finished and still had the trip to the pet warehouse to undertake.

The whole day has been foggy, a very heavy mist that has hung like a dirty white curtain across the whole of the garden and completely blocked the views of the hills. We wound our way around the country lanes in the fog and fading light and arrived at the warehouse. It is manned by a really friendly team of men who joke and laugh their way through whatever chore they are working at. We finished our shopping and they loaded up our car for us without having to be asked and told us to take care and thanked us for visiting. On the way back we stopped as the view was amazing. The hills were separated by the mist. A sheer white blanket just laid between the hills and the fields.

So eventually home and time to put the chickens to bed. They had all decided to sit on the wooden plank we had erected for them and as I got into the dovecote I could barely see them. I could hear them though and as I reached out to grab one the noise increased. Fortunately I managed to get all three, one after another, and tuck them safely into bed so to speak. Next time I'll take a torch! We have head lamps to wear as the night time here is pitch black; they are extremely handy to have as it leaves both hands free.

We have never been so busy. That old adage 'how did I find time to work?' is actually true, although this move has proven to be life-changing. We are more active and eat and sleep better (when I am not snoring, that is) and all in all it really is a very different way of life.

The familiar sound of dogs waking up, shaking their heads causing their ears to flap loudly against each other is always the first thing we hear. It almost sounds as though they are applauding the sun for rising and giving them another day to be spoiled, chase birds, trip us up and generally cause havoc.

As usual it was dark when I took them out first thing, but the lawn was covered in a thick white frost that glowed in the fading swansong of light from the moon. It was lovely to walk them at this time and I felt a complete inner peace which was matched by the lack of noise around me. That was until Phoebe clocked a barn owl flying boldly past the end of the garden. For me it was a wondrous sight, for Phoebe it was an early breakfast if she could just get at it and jump about twenty feet in the air. Regardless of the impossible odds on her catching the owl she decided it was worth a punt and took off with me on the end of the lead. Meantime Flo, who hasn't got a hunting gene in her body, decided if it was good enough for Phoebe it was good enough for her, the only difference being Flo hadn't got a clue why she was doing what she was doing. So despite the complete lack of comprehension she also took off in the same direction and the second re-run of the Ben-Hur chariot scene ensued. The only way I could stop them was to dig my heels in the ground and turn around to drag them the other way, both frantically barking and frothing at the mouth. This set Trevor's dogs off and by half past seven the whole of the area was awake. All this and I hadn't even had a cup of tea yet.

Today was my first visit to my new GP. I arrived nice and early while Helen had a wander around the shops. It's a nice surgery with two televisions in the waiting area both showing the same woman with a burning hole in her forehead and a droopy mouth to one side. I watched it once but by the eighth time I got a little bored and turned to my phone for amusement. My appointment was at 11:10am and they had booked a double as it was my first consultation. At 11:05am I was called in. I nearly became very disorientated due to the shock of being called early but managed to stagger to the right door. My GP introduced himself and proceed to get a potted history from me. I was so pleased he was the one GP that had a special interest in rheumatology and he listened intently and between us looked at my current drug regime and made some changes. All in all, a successful visit. During this time Helen had come back into the surgery and just before I had been called in another patient who was called into another GP couldn't get up off their chair. Helen being Helen got up and helped him, resulting in her pulling her already fragile back even further. She is now in pain but being her usual stoic self she is trying to pretend all is well. We play this game now and then it goes like this: Helen hurts her back and starts walking with bandy legs and a slight sideways gait. I notice and ask if she has hurt her back. She says it is fine and nothing is wrong, ignoring the fact that I have seen this hundreds of times before and also as a retired nurse of long standing I have a slight idea regarding reading the signs of a hurty back. She is now lying on her side on the couch as I write and still pretending.

This afternoon we pottered in the garden, Helen stoically still trying to walk normally, meanwhile Phoebe made it her mission to cross the stream to get to the hens; still no eggs, by the way. I repaired the wire fencing I had put up over one bridge, but instinct and determination on Phoebe's part was no match for my pathetic human endeavours. At one point she was swimming up the stream in full view of Helen and I standing open-mouthed watching her. When we found a way to stop her crossing the stream she found another escape route through the barred fencing which we now have to put yet another load of stock fencing on. Helen is of the opinion that whatever we do she will find a way; meantime it's chickens out and dogs in. I think we need a proper fence right across that side of the garden. Helen thinks it will spoil the look of it. Watch this space.

CHAPTER 11

The sound of a tractor roaring up and down the lane at around 9 o'clock in the morning made us both walk outside to see what was occurring. It was Trevor on his tractor lawnmower. A big tractor lawnmower. Trevor asked if we wanted to try it out. As we had owned a smaller model before when we lived in Old Heathfield I declined as I didn't fancy having my sore joints jiggled up and down but Helen could not resist and was riding around in her little red hat like Noddy. She was in her element.

We decided that we had to find our local rubbish tip as the rubbish is piling up and for the sake of our mental health it needs to be gone. The tip itself is a strange affair. In order to get there it's a twelve-mile drive albeit through winding country lanes and fields dotted with sheep looking like balls of cotton wool on the horizon. The odd red kite flies overhead as do the buzzards, looking for rodents or smaller birds that have taken their eye off the ball momentarily. According to Trevor one of his pigeons fell foul of a red kite in his garden. The jury is out on that one!

On our twelve-mile journey we passed about three cars so it was a busy day today. We had leftover rubbish from the move in addition to the household stuff and having yet again missed the bin day a trip to this establishment was sorely needed. We arrived at the dump and never a more appropriate name has ever been given to a place. In

Worthing, the 'tip' was organised like a military operation. Each large skip there was labelled clearly in bold typing on large overhead signs to let you know what you could put in them. The cars lined up patiently awaiting the next space to drive into. There were skips for cardboard, paper, metal, plastics etc. etc. This 'tip' has about four skips in all with either cardboard or wooden signs that someone had written in ineligible writing informing us what should go in them. These signs hang skewed to one side as though they have given up caring or actually never cared to begin with. Cars came in at speed and parked wherever they liked. The rule is that only two black sacks can be disposed of at any one time; pleading newcomer ignorance we got away with four. Our recycling which we have to put in blue bags, means we have to sort the cardboard from the cans, plastic etc. We gave up on that one and brought the blue bags home to put in our little rubbish hut made of wood. Our wooden hut is surviving by the skin of its teeth, it is so old. It reminds me of the till in 'Open All Hours' – once you get the lid up it wants to close so you take your life in your hands trying to prise it open and then letting it shut without amputating your arm. Anyway the blue bags and their contents went for a nice twenty-four mile round trip before being dumped unceremoniously in the knackered wooden receptacle. Driving away totally underwhelmed by this experience we decided to go to Sainsbury's as Trevor and Jill are coming for drinks and nibbles Sunday night. We trooped around throwing various items into our trolley and happy with our purchases made our way home.

Helen pottered in the garden; the weather was really cold again but the bright sunshine led us to believe it was warmer than it actually was. Red kites as always were overhead and their strange whistle-type call is a constant background noise here at Ty Mawr. There are worse things. I decided to get on with some much-needed housework, while Helen was in the garden with Flo and Phoebe. Phoebe left the chickens alone mostly today as Trevor's guinea fowl were rampaging up and down the lane. Evidently they are better than guard dogs noise-wise. They do make one hell of a racket and Phoebe at one point managed to squeeze her nose through the stock wire fencing so far she resembled a canine version of Pinocchio. Helen escorted her indoors to save any further pandemonium.

I had just finished my chores when there was a knock on the door. Trevor and Thomas were standing there. Trevor explained that

Thomas's bottom milk tooth was hanging on by a thread and his hands were too big to put into Thomas's mouth to pull the tooth out – could I do it? I asked Thomas if that's what he wanted me to do and faced with the prospect of the Tooth Fairy visiting that night he readily agreed. He sat on my lap and I inspected the task before me. This tiny little milk tooth that sat in the middle of his lower jaw at the front was the first ever tooth he had lost so this occasion was a momentous one in Thomas's short life. Armed with tissue and my delicate lady fingers I tugged away at the tooth which was tougher to come out than it looked. I could see that he would be unable to eat properly with running the risk of swallowing it either then or in his sleep, so I persevered and pop! Out it came. Thomas's little face was a joy with a grin from ear to ear. He is a tough kid, not once wincing or complaining. I just went to offer him some sweets for being so brave when Trevor told me he had been naughty at school that day so no TV and no sweets. I guess given the fact I had just pulled a tooth out offering sweets was entirely inappropriate anyway.

So here we are again in front of our burner enjoying the delight of dry logs and moaning about the stupid storylines of EastEnders. We have decided on the fencing to prevent the dogs getting at the hens. Fred is coming back tomorrow to give us a quote. It will be a relief to get that sorted out for both us and the chickens.

Silly as it sounds the weekend still feels like a time to relax even though we are retired. Having said that, we do work quite hard during the week at present, constantly finding things to do. This morning things found us.

Lying in bed reading with a cup of tea at about 08:30 we were startled by an almighty crash from somewhere downstairs. It was loud, loud enough to make Helen think the ceiling had come down in the kitchen. Rushing down the stairs, Flo and Phoebe hanging back in case it was something scary, we found that the radiator in the kitchen had fallen off the wall and water was leaking from the two joints either end. Now we knew that the radiator was a problem as it was loose, not loose enough for us to think that it would collapse but it was something we took on board as a 'must be fixed' thought. The wall is plaster board and the rawl plugs they had used were totally inadequate. We pushed the radiator back up to its original position but one of us had to stay there holding it unless we wanted a repeat performance. Helen held it while I got my very heavy, enormous holdall that all my tools are in and turning it up on its side manage to wedge the radiator against the wall, freeing Helen up. The water though was starting to become serious and I now know why Tupperware containers are essential, they were just the right size to put under the pipes each end to catch the flow of water.

I rang Trevor. Down he came with Thomas in tow wearing his Teletubby hat this time, and asked where the stopcock was. We didn't have a scooby where to look so I set off on a stopcock hunt, firstly outside and then inside. Trevor in the meantime tightened up the nuts on the pipework to try and stop the flow. Eventually both he and I decided to look behind the dishwasher for the stopcock and there it was. I have never been so happy to see a metal tap in all my life. After having turned it off Trevor removed the radiator but gallons of black water proceeded to pour out of the pipes which galvanised us all into battle stations mode. Thomas was sitting at the table eating toast and jam and watching all of this with great amusement.

'Water's on the floor,' he informed us several times.

'It's black too.'

We thanked him for this insight and carried on running around the kitchen emptying Tupperware containers as though there was no tomorrow. By now, the floor, the skirting, the walls and the pathway to the sink resembled a scene from the film 'Creature from the Black Lagoon'. Finally the ink stopped flowing and we started Operation Clean-up. In the meantime Trevor had gone to Williams builders' merchants and bought the caps for the pipes and also got the number of a plumber, Owain. Trevor and Thomas left once Trevor had capped off the pipes and once again we thanked him profusely. He has found a new nickname for us, by the way, it's 'the two silly cows across the way'. Apt.

Owain arrived within half an hour and we had decided to get rid of the radiator as the kitchen was always warm with the oven and the other radiator on the other side. Trevor got rid of all the pipework, reset the boiler, bled all the radiators upstairs and down, sorted out the poor flush on the loo and after about an hour and a half we were dreading the Saturday call-out bill. Bracing myself, I asked how much.

'Is £60 alright with you?' he asked.

I nearly did a happy dance! Alright? It was fan-bloody-tastic! Owain is only a young man but knew his stuff and was thorough. It took me back to the time when in Worthing I had to call a plumber out to fix a leaking tap. After he had charged me £65 for the two ceramic washers that he said were needed, he couldn't get the taps off to mend it and then charged me £125 call-out fee on a weekday.

Once Helen and I cleared up the mess from the kitchen it was already early afternoon. We hadn't showered, had breakfast or achieved anything other than feed the dogs and let the hens out. The weather was horrid. Rain, dreary and so cold. We decided it was a stay indoors day, or what was left of it.

So now we have a bare wall with holes in it, soon mended with Polyfilla and some emulsion paint, we hope. In addition we have room now for another unit to give me some badly needed drawer space.

So that was today, the fun never ends.

The next day saw no radiators falling off the wall, no dogs chasing chickens or escaping. No torrential rain or snow. In fact very little occurred. That was until this evening.

After having decided what to do about the Phoebe vs Chickens problem we had Fred come around today to measure up and advise us as to price etc. We are having two farm gates put in to divide the garden into two. One side will be the 'business' end with the vegetable plot, stream, chickens and mini orchard and bees. The other side will be the pretty flowery part. It will mean that Phoebe the Huntress will be foiled in her quest to desecrate the chicken population of Ty Mawr. Well, that's the plan. I have never known a dog so hell bent on the destruction of anything that dares to be within the borders of her territory. So the gates hopefully will solve our problem.

This evening we had invited Trevor and Jill for drinks and nibbles. I prepared some onion bhajis and chicken tikka bites along with the usual dips etc. They arrived and the evening progressed into slight mayhem. Helen and Trevor are best mates and end up laughing at their own jokes that progressively get worse as the alcohol increases. Jill and I did our best to ignore them and have an intelligent conversation but it proved difficult with them two dancing (and I use the term very loosely) in front of us to Tom Jones's greatest hits. Trevor's dancing needs to be experienced to be believed. I'm not quite sure how long it will take me to get the mental image out of my brain but with the right counselling a full recovery may be achieved. The saddest part is, Helen, who can usually bust some moves, ended up copying him so we were treated to a double dose of the spectacle. Jill told me of the time she took him early on in their relationship to a pub and due to Trevor's limp-wristed boogie he ended up being propositioned several times by various men. Trevor hadn't got a clue why they wanted him to go to the loo with them.

In addition to this visual carnage the choice of music equalled it. I have never been a huge fan of the Jones music although I like the man. It's never been a genre of music that I have enjoyed, however, after tonight I have come to the conclusion I hate it. If I ever hear 'Delilah' or 'The Green, Green Grass of Home' again I may spontaneously combust. They enjoyed themselves but I do have a feeling both of them may feel slightly under par in the morning. Gin, wine and champagne was consumed in vast quantities. I'm so glad I am teetotal. Jill asked if she could leave Trevor here but decided to just prop him up against their wall for the night instead.

So we got to bed at 12:30am which for those of you that know us well is about three hours after our usual bedtime. The dogs have got the hump with us as we kept them in the kitchen and conservatory and they felt excluded. I can't even get Flo to talk to me, she just averts her big brown eyes every time I approach and breathes a huge sob-like sigh. Phoebe took herself off to her bed, slamming the door behind her.

I think they are upset.

CHAPTER 12

As predicted, Helen was feeling less than motivated the day after the evening before. She stoically struggled on doing the usual everyday stuff we all have to do, like breathe, dress, eat etc. However, I could tell by looking at her that each chore was taking an immense effort to achieve. I heard her at one point saying to herself, 'Just do one thing and rest.'

That's how bad it was.

I do recall with hindsight Helen taking the dogs out before we went to bed and becoming concerned that she was a long time given her inebriated condition. She finally fell through the back door, dogs in tow, and I heard her shouting my name in little weak voice. When I got to the door she was standing there with her headlamp on over her woolly hat and the hood of her coat over that. Somehow the headlamp straps had completely twisted around her head and covered her eyes with the torch bit shining up her nose. I have to admit to straining to keep my full bladder under control because I was laughing so much. She managed to get herself free without my help as I was too weak with laughter to sort it out.

I had to inject my methotrexate for my RA before going to bed. For those who don't know the drug it is usually used in cancer treatment, however, it has been found in much smaller doses to relieve in some part, the devastating effects RA can have on the joints and therefore preventing the awful deformity this disease used to cause. I remember treating patients who had RA and some of them could no longer use their hands as the joints had completely been destroyed by the inflammation.

Sometimes I just get tired the next day and sleep more than usual, sometimes I may be nauseous. I have been told it depends on my blood levels etc. when I inject. This time the effects were quite debilitating. I woke up feeling dreadful and all I wanted to do was sleep. The nausea was coming over me in waves so I had to take pills to stop it. To cut a long story short I slept for hours, waking at about 2pm. I forced myself out of bed and showered only to sleep my way through the evening, the night and most of Tuesday. However, I am up now, showered once more and know the worst is over. I still feel a bit nauseous and my joints are all having a pain party but I don't feel wiped out so onwards and upwards.

So now I am back in the land of the living, not feeling one hundred percent but running at roughly seventy percent. I am sitting here in the lounge in front of our log fire listening to the wind whistling outside and down the chimney, every now and again catching the flames in the fire and breathing new life into them. There is something so comforting about a log fire especially when the weather outside is bitter, although I must say it does feel like the opening scene of a Hammer House horror film at times, especially when I look in the mirror.

The next day recovered sufficiently to report that I am nearly back to my old self which although not great, is normal for me.

I had to go to the surgery in Llanfwr this morning for my monthly blood test and as we were getting the car out of our drive and shutting the farm gate I noticed the cardboard and the black sacks holding our rubbish were missing. Having been out of action for two days I thought to myself what a good job Helen had done getting rid of it all.

So we trundled to the surgery and as we had cut it fine leaving I was a little late. I sat waiting for five minutes and then got called into the phlebotomist and no sooner had I rolled up my sleeve the tourniquet was on and my blood had been drawn. It was the fastest blood test I have ever had. I almost left before I arrived. That done, we walked around for a while and found this shop called Toast.

It sells arty-farty clothes for women, very stylish but very expensive. Helen got herself a lovely linen top in their sale but there wasn't anything in there I particular wanted, or needed for that matter.

My youngest son is forty next week. My baby. I can hardly believe it. So that's all three in their forties. Do I feel old? You bet your life I do!

I decided to do some housework this afternoon as the weather is bitter and evidently snow is expected in some areas. Helen loves being outside and made herself busy out in the garden. Trevor and Jill drove past and informed Helen they had taken all our rubbish to the tip. So that's where it went! What we failed to realise was there was at least two weeks' doggie dooings in bags amongst it all which made their trip to Lampeter refuse disposal site less that fragrant.

'It stunk, bud,' he said. 'Even the young guy working there took a step back when he hauled the bag out of the trailer. It was bloody awful, bud.'

They were laughing, thank goodness. Helen was horrified and gasped when she was confronted with this awful reality, and when she came in to tell me I didn't know whether to laugh or cry so I laughed. I could just imagine their faces on their drive across the lovely green fields and valleys with a swarm of bluebottles in tow and the putrid smell of dog poo emanating from the back of their truck. We are going to have to find something else to do with the poo. A Doggie Dooley is the answer. We will have to invest in a digest(er).

We are thinking of having the worktops in the kitchen replaced; the units are fine, just need a change of handles, but the worktops have seen better days, so I am looking forward to giving it a facelift.

We have also ordered a greenhouse which the lovely Steve is going to put up for us and it means another visit from him and Carol which is the best part. We need the greenhouse so we can start off our seedlings and start the self-sufficiency we promised ourselves. Really cannot wait to get all our plans into action. Steve is a genius at DIY and the pair of them are two of the most generous people we know. We are so lucky with our friends. There is a queue forming to come and visit; it's great that everyone wants to see us. It makes us happy and grateful.

After the howling gale-force winds of last night the garden

resembled a post-apocalyptic scene from a movie. Our metal, heavy swing seat ended up halfway down the garden and the amount of branches from the trees that had been ripped from their base will at least make good firewood once dry.

I ventured over to the hens and wondered if today was the day they would start to earn their keep. But nothing. I am beginning to think they know what a good thing they are onto having full board, living in a Grade II listed dovecote, with corn on tap, grit, water and pellets, crap everywhere and do nothing in return. A bit similar to having a sixteen-year-old in the house. I had a firm word with them but I think it's falling on deaf ears. They dismissed my rantings with a wave of their wing, walked straight past me into their pen and started eating their free three-course breakfast. I retreated knowing that behind my back they were giving me the chicken equivalent of 'the finger'.

Helen spent the day in Llandovery with Trevor. He was going there and invited us both along. I wasn't up to a day walking around to be honest so decided to stay here and just enjoy my surroundings. I fed the wild birds and dodged the raindrops in between. Spoke to the company who are going to install the new work surfaces and sorted out the survey. Before all this can happen we have to remove the tiles in the kitchen. So all the necessary tools needed to complete this have been ordered from Amazon – tile chisel, sander, tile adhesive remover, face masks and eye googles. Girl power. I will let you know how we get on and what hospital we are being cared for in due course.

Helen returned home with two beef bones for the dogs. Flo and Phoebe instinctively know when one of us has decided to treat them and made straight for the bag; actually I think their sense of smell may have played a small part. Bones given, they fell on them and the carnage ensued. Helen hadn't had lunch so she decided to gorge herself on a full bag of Bombay mix. So there I was in the living room, Flo sitting next to me grinding away at the bone, Phoebe with her razor-sharp teeth and incredible jaw strength cracking away, taking chunks out of it as if it were marshmallow and then Helen, eating Bombay mix as though there was no tomorrow and her munching was surpassing the safe decibel threshold recommended for the human ear. I was genuinely worried I was at risk of permanent hearing loss. After enduring this assault on the ear drums for about twenty minutes I casually mentioned to Helen that she may ruin her dinner if she carried on eating in the hope she may stop, but she felt she would be fine. I bit my lip and stoically sat quietly in silent torment and finally she stopped. I'm still twitching now and again and my tinnitus is at an all-time high but hopefully it will pass.

Friday was a busy day. The shed, or potting shed as it is now was chock-a-block with the excess stuff we had taken out the house. Some removal boxes remained, bags of things that would be attended to later were left abandoned on the dusty floor and bags upon bags of paper needed for the fire waited patiently to be used.

We set about trying to bring some order to this and having two chests of drawers that can be used helped. I managed to separate the gardening items from car boot items (we have been going to do one for nine years now) and then miscellaneous stuff that neither of us know what to do with.

When we had finished the shed actually looked presentable but what we had done was to put everything we didn't want from the shed into the garage. So guess what our next job is? It is hard to move in the garage now. Monday will see us making our way over vale and hill with more rubbish for the Lampeter tip, what joy! This is fast becoming our social event of the week. OK, let me rephrase that, this is our social event of the week… Or is it?

Saturday, and in the village hall in the next village is the monthly Farmers' Market. Thrilled at the prospect of meeting more neighbours and mingling amongst the crowd buying locally grown wares and homemade cakes, we rose early and got ourselves ready. As this was a big occasion I put on my new lambswool jumper, a present from Helen at Christmas, and we both looked presentable, we thought. Trevor had knocked earlier and said he was going. 'Get there early,' he advised.

Fearing we would miss all the bargains we did as we were told and made our way there in good time. It took us about a four-minute drive and we duly parked in the small village hall car park and noticed we were about the sixth car there. Feeling gratified and a bit smug that we had beaten the early onslaught we made our way into the hall.

Picture the scene. In the middle of this small hall were four long wooden tables. Two were empty, one had three bits of cheese on it and a sprig of rosemary and the other one was piled up with locally grown vegetables covered in mud.

At the end of the hall was an urn, billowing steam from the water that it was obviously boiling, a plateful of mixed biscuits were proudly displayed alongside a jam roll and on the stage a woman in a woolly hat and fingerless gloves was frying bacon on a portable camping stove. A sign read:

Tea and Coffee 50p

Bacon sandwich £1.50

Biscuits and ketchup free

Trevor was already there drinking coffee. Helen joined him and had a cup but I declined the tea and coffee. I only drink Earl Grey and I had a sneaking suspicion they wouldn't have any. Coffee gives me thumping headaches, so I was happy to go without. We all sat down at one of the spare tables and I was beginning to feel overdressed and wished I'd kept my pyjamas on, it wouldn't have looked out of place.

Trevor announced the cake table was late due to unforeseen circumstances and as his sole reason for going there was to purchase a Victoria sponge so he had to sit it out. I decided to do the decent thing and have a look round the two tables and thirty seconds later I was back with three dirty parsnips, two garlic cloves and an onion.

Suddenly there was a commotion at the top empty table and a woman in a headscarf carrying a tray full of cakes clattered into the room at which point Trevor went into battle stations mode. Flying across the hall, he wasted no time securing his quest and made his way back pleased as punch holding a Victoria sandwich like a posh butler holds a drinks tray. He had such a satisfied look on his face I have vowed to make him a Victoria sandwich for next weekend as he has another four weeks to wait until a repeat performance of this major spectacular.

Helen and I made our way home and as usual the dogs acted as though we had been gone a fortnight.

The weather is damp, raining and after the excitement of this morning we felt a peaceful afternoon was the order of the day. We think we have a family of otters living in the river nearby. Trevor reckons they are mink but Helen has seen it on two occasions now and she thinks it is too big to be a mink and its face is rounder like an otter, so who knows? My lovely daughter Louise is coming for a week or so this coming Wednesday and she will be thrilled if she could see one and no doubt clarify what it is. She has an extraordinary talent for identifying wildlife. If I get stuck trying to name a moth, bird etc. I send the photo to Lou and low and behold within a short time she has nailed it. Can't wait.

CHAPTER 13

I signed up for warnings and flood alerts from the Natural Resource Centre of Wales to let me know if there are any possibilities of floods in our area. We are about 150 yards from the banks of the river and also have a large stream in our garden. Yesterday saw relentless, torrential downpours all day long. Helen had decided to go with Jill and Trevor to a nursery to look at some plants, I decided they were mad and stayed in to assemble our new acquisition of a kitchen cabinet that will give us more cupboard and drawer space.

At about half past two the phone rang and a recorded voice told me that we were to 'Be Aware' that floods were likely in our area. I looked out the kitchen window as I had been engrossed in this cabinet and saw that the stream was fit to burst and the stone banks could not be seen as the water had passed them.

Deciding not to worry as the cottage has never been flooded since 1860, I gainly carried on hitting my fingers with a hammer, crushing my hands between pieces of wood and dropping heavy objects on my feet. I ended up with a black nail as a result of a crush injury which obviously I still have and will admit it was a tad painful. It throbbed all night and is still very tender this morning. Helen, Jill and Trevor arrived back absolutely wet through and telling me not to panic? Trevor went off and dug a trench to enable the water from the stream on the lane to flow more freely. We sat around and chatted for a while and when they left I finished off the cabinet and finally the rain stopped. The water levels go down very quickly. One minute they look a bit ominous and the next they are back to normal.

A very relaxed evening followed and an early night which is just as well as Phoebe got us up twice with a stomach upset. She is such a clean girl and how she held onto it goodness only knows, it was that bad. So consequently at 02:30am and 5:00am we were both up and walking around the garden. How pleasant.

The next day saw us not bright or very happy due to lack of sleep; we eventually had to drag ourselves out of bed. Gwen, our postie, called with a parcel and the usual dog biscuits. It was still raining albeit lightly. We were going to go back to the nursery as Helen was really impressed with it but my GP was going to phone me about some dodgy blood test results so I had to wait in. It turned out my liver enzymes are raised but it's due to the methotrexate so I have to go back to see the GP soon. I'm not worried, it will get sorted.

I think the chickens are starting to feel more settled now as we have done our best to keep the dogs away from them and when we finally get these gates up we will all feel better, especially the chickens. One day if we are very, very lucky they might lay an egg!

So back to today. Helen spent the day in the garden in its entirety. She adores it out there. I was out there for a while helping out. One of the jobs was to ensure the stream was flowing properly into the next field and eventually back into the river. There were some weeds and reeds that had gathered into a bit of a mess but it's easily remedied with the help of a grass rake. I did have visions of falling in and the thought was less than pleasant.

Helen was chatting to Trevor over the fence at the bottom amongst a gaggle of geese that he owns. They make the most amazing noises and strangely enough Phoebe and Flo ignore them now. Helen happened to mention that one of the large round rock garden features we have has a tree stump covered in ivy in the middle of it and they both came up with the idea that if Trevor used his chainsaw to make a deep well in the middle of the stump, Helen could fill it with soil and have an enormous fern growing out of it. She also is going to remove the euphorbia plants in it as Jill will have these and then fill in the surrounding area with her beloved iris rhizomes. It will look lovely. What she didn't count on was when

Trevor stood on top of the rockery and started to saw into it, the resulting sawdust emanating from it completely covered her new car (the mother ship). The look on her face was wonderful. I knew straight away that inside she was imploding but she stayed looking calm with a fixed smile on her face. At one point I thought she was going to pass out with angst but she held it together. The sight of her this afternoon vacuuming the outside of the car was unusual to say the least. If I had covered it in sawdust what remained of me would be floating in the Cothi by now.

We have another busy(ish) couple of weeks ahead. We have another wonderful trip to the Lampeter tip to look forward to, the scrap iron merchants to sell the radiator that committed suicide when it fell off our wall. Helen has the dentist, I have the GP and Lou is due Wednesday. We are picking her up from Swansea. My eldest son and his wife are coming Sunday for lunch which will be lovely, and then we have the kitchen tiles to demolish when Lou has gone home.

Life is treating us very well of late. The initial stress of moving and adjusting has levelled out to an acceptable stage now and we have stopped thinking we are on holiday and have started to realise we live here and that's wonderful.

I nearly did not get to write this.

As previously told we had the kamikaze radiator to dispose of and prior to Helen's dental appointment decided to get this done on our way there. So with co-ordinates set into our trusty sat nav we proceeded on our merry way. We had left late so were pushing it a bit time wise even by our standards. Well, Helen's, I am always punctual. Helen on the other hand has no concept of time. However, we did run out of time and also got lost even with the sat nav's directions. I do wonder about her at times, the sat nav woman, I mean. She sometimes sends us very wrong, taking the longest route possible especially here in Wales where we are guided through tiny lanes and people's kitchens to get to our destination. Is she menopausal? Is something going on in her private life I know nothing about and she gainly carries on telling the nation of the geographically challenged the right roads to travel? So we turned around and made our way back to Llanfwr. On the opposite side of the road a large articulated lorry was coming towards us when all of a sudden a car appeared from behind it on our side of the road and was coming at breakneck speed threatening to hit us head-on. Helen slowed right down, the lorry slowed down and the moron in the car just managed to miss us by feet. The lorry driver flashed and tooted and I gave the driver 'the finger'. Helen turned to me and in the calmest voice possible said, 'That was close, wasn't it?'

This statement has now been entered into the National Understatements of the Year Awards 2018.

We both confessed afterwards that we thought our time was up and it took about ten minutes for my heart to actually go back into sinus rhythm.

We got into Llanfwr still shaking our heads in disbelief and Helen trotted off to the dentist and I went to the bank and had a general wander around. The bank was shut so I wandered around for a while, popping into the Salvation Army charity shop where is was full to the rafters with various unwanted items and a bored woman flicked through a magazine at the counter. Leaving there, I went to the florist and bought some daffodils to be patriotic.

I sat in the car waiting for Helen and she turned up shortly afterwards. After a quick chat with Lou on the phone we drove home.

Trevor has bought a rusty suit of armour (don't ask) and it now stands in front of his wall facing us as we drive down the lane. It's called Raymondo. He said he got it to protect his property and 'keep the gays out'. So we are going to one night sneak along and put a straw hat on it, a dress and handbag. Can't wait to see his face when he takes Thomas to school and drives past it the next morning.

The weather like the rest of the country is appalling at the moment. The wind has been dreadful and being in a valley we get it full pelt. Couple that with the rain and it can be really fun here.

So the next day dawned and we set off to get Lou. She started her journey by train in Eastbourne at 8:04, changed at Brighton and thought to reach Bristol Parkway before finally getting the train from there to Swansea where we would meet her.

All was going swimmingly until she got to Westbury Station in Wiltshire where the train stopped and carried on stopping for over an hour. She was told there was no driver, then it was the wrong type of rain. Then after this she was put onto another train and then again told there was no driver. Seems like Great Western Railways are in the same state as all the others.

Obviously we had left at the arranged time to pick Lou up so finding she had been delayed gave us some extras shopping time.

Our first stop was M&S Food Hall. Helen could hardly contain her excitement, a proper shop! Obviously we realised we couldn't buy anything frozen in case we didn't get it home in good time but undeterred she soldiered on; she managed to satiate some of her retail addiction with bottles of wine, crisps, a loaf of bread and other bits and pieces. After lunch in there also we moved on the Pets at Home for dog food and bird food, followed by Poundland and Laura Ashley. Eclectic shopping is us!

After killing enough time we ventured onto the mayhem of Swansea's road system which is somewhat scary. One ways, triple junctions, traffic lights all in the most unsuspecting places and bus lanes galore. Eventually we got to the station car park with twenty minutes to spare. Swansea station only has about half a dozen platforms and we found out we needed platform two. After a wait in came the train and off stepped Lou looking remarkably well and refreshed after an eight-hour trip.

We had worked out the dogs had been on their own for about five hours now and started to worry in case they needed a pee or even worse a poo! We needn't have worried. Apart from going ballistic at our homecoming, nothing had been chewed, peed or pooed on. The chickens were put away, the dinner was started, dogs fed and Louise unpacked and settled. It is so nice to have her here. I think she was a bit shocked as to the remoteness of the area but loved the hills and views that surround the cottage. She looked forward to a proper look tomorrow.

We have planned a trip to see the red kites feeding and also to the Botanical Gardens of Wales where they have an abundance of tropical butterflies, flowers and flora. We will also show her the delights of Llanfwr, warning her not to blink in case she misses it.

I find it hard to write when I have guests here. Having said that, more actually goes on than when it's just Helen and myself.

Unfortunately the weather hasn't been wonderful for Louise's visit. Thursday saw us generally catching up on news and showing her the gardens and house. She, like us, is mad about wildlife so she was very happy with the abundance of birds that come and go in the garden.

We have lots of feeders thanks partly to Steve. The most popular being the pine cone one. He fixed pine cones onto a piece of wood with their cones facing outward and then we come along and smother it in peanut butter and the birds go wild for it. It is especially popular with smaller birds. The other popular ones are the fat ball feeders left by our predecessors. These are just ceramic half spheres with a circular wire other half that screws onto it with the fat ball well encased and squirrel-proof. We have squirrels of course and they get plenty to eat off the tables.

Louise and I took a walk with Trevor and Jill around their garden and Lou took lots of photos of his various fowl and assortment of strange-looking chickens; one in particular is a turkey-necked hen. Odd to look at. Speaking of hens, no eggs. We have been given a false egg to put into their box to try and flip their laying switch on, so to speak. It hasn't worked so far, they just look bemused as to what it is doing there and what it's supposed to be.

Yesterday turned out to be gloriously sunny and quite oddly warm. Making the most of the big yellow thing in the sky, Lou and I went over to the red kite feeding centre on the edge of the Brecon Beacons. I had told Louise about this spectacular display but I think she was not expecting what she saw. We were only two of about six people there and the chap who runs it fed the birds twice ensuring he placed it in our line of vision so we could get some good shots. These magnificent birds are so quick, photographing them is a challenge. They soar overhead silently and nonchalantly as though thoroughly disinterested in the meat below them and then suddenly from nowhere you hear the wind rushing past you and a 'swish' sound and the bird has taken its fare and is making its way skyward again. It truly was a wonderful time to share with Louise and I could tell she was awestruck.

The journey home was a little scary. The roads to the centre are just more or less one-way tracks that pass little smallholdings and farms abutting the road directly. On our way past one such place a small Jack Russell terrier decided to try and kill itself by running under the front of my car. Fortunately I screeched to a halt just in time. The ungrateful little sod couldn't care less that I had just prevented it from a gruesome death and carried yapping at me at the side of my door. Inching away from it, I managed a getaway. Within ten minutes a blue-eyed sheepdog decided to do exactly the same thing with the same outcome, I am pleased to say, but it did leave me questioning whether this was a deliberate conspiracy on behalf of the dog world, possibly demonstrating against not being fed enough titbits or wanting the right to vote. Personally I would give them the right to vote, they couldn't do any worse than the humans have done in recent elections.

Today we saw rain again. We had planned to go out this evening for a meal in one of the community-run pubs where people take turns in cooking. The pub is also a shop and a post office. The pub only opens at 7pm each night and it is cash only. Good for them, I say; at least they have been enterprising enough to keep their pub open and their community spirit intact. We decided not to go out as both Lou and I were feeling less than well. We did go to the 'Two Soups' café though and had a light lunch. I noticed whilst in there my leather gloves that I lost before Christmas. I asked the owner when they had been found and our stories matched so I have them back! As I was leaving I left behind the other leather gloves I was wearing that day and had to go back for them. At least it proved I was completely capable of leaving leather gloves wherever I visited.

Today being Holocaust Memorial Day, we watched a couple of programmes on the subject. Even though I have read extensively about this horrific period of history and watched dozens of documentaries and films, I never become complacent regarding the devastating reality of the inhumanity that occurred. I still draw breath with sheer abhorrence listening to recounts of the suffering that was inflicted and endured. No, we should never forget. But do we learn?

As previously mentioned a few times it's a bit wet here and finding stuff to do amongst the rain, hail and torrential downpours can be challenging.

This morning, although not bucketing down, it was that fine drizzle that leads you into thinking it's not that bad until you spend half an hour in it and realise you are wet through. Undeterred, we decided to visit Talley Lakes which are about a mile and a half from our cottage and supposed to be abundant in wildlife, water fowl and the likes. There are also the abbey ruins there which make for a very atmospheric setting when the day is dull and misty.

So off we trotted full of expectation on the adventure that lay ahead. Armed with camera, binoculars and for some reason a pear each to stave off starvation (Helen's idea).

When we got there we looked for the pathway that was on the website that would guide us gently around the lakes, leading us to a hide so we could eat our pears indoors and generally have a nice stroll. Can you see where this is going?

We got through the gate onto the field that leads down to the lakes only to find we had embarked on a bit of a challenge. When I say challenge I mean a route march in conditions only SAS recruits would attempt to undertake and then under duress.

The mud was thick and relentless. Each footstep was like plunging into quicksand. We walked along trying desperately to find a foothold that would not necessarily mean we would end up being sucked under into the chasms of hell. Helen strode ahead like some sort of Girl Guide leader determined to overcome the obstacles that lay in her path.

We had just reached the end of the first lake when I noticed Helen was struggling to get her foot out of the mud; she had sunk quite a bit and she said afterwards the ground around her was moving indicating it was very unstable.

Louise and I found the same only it was just me that was stuck. Vainly trying to help me, she held tightly onto my arm as I strained to release the grip the mud had on my boot. Finally with a gargantuan effort my boot became free and as I tried to straighten myself up Louise lost her balance and in slow motion she started to tumble backwards into the mire still gripping tightly onto my arm. The inevitable happened. I fell too, landing partly on poor old Lou and partly side-on into the sludge-like muck. We both laid there for a second repeating, 'You OK?' about five times before deciding how we were going to get up causing minimal damage and mess. The first thing that had to come off were the gloves we were wearing as they were absolutely soaked in mud and dripping. We both looked like Mud Monsters only worse. Louise struggled to her feet and I followed; neither of us would have graduated from finishing school with our poise and deportment. By this time Helen had seen what had happened and was wading her way towards us. At this point we all felt it may be best to go home. The mud and water was running down the inside of my trousers and I could feel my pants had begun to take on an entirely different shape to what they should be. Louise was worse off; the mud hung heavily from her jeans and coat and with that and the rain soaking us, we felt slightly uncomfortable.

We got back to the car all agreeing it was the stupidest idea since Mr Hitler said to Mrs Hitler, 'Let's have a baby.' I took off my coat, turned it inside out and sat on it. Helen produced an empty wild bird food plastic sack from the boot and Louise spent the ride home sat on this.

We got home and stripped off in search of warm clothes and a wash. Once we had sorted ourselves out I examined the damage to the cameras and binoculars. Fortunately we had both had the sense to protect them as we fell so the mud hadn't infiltrated any of the lenses etc. The only things that did escape being covered in mud was a parking ticket from yesterday and a tampon Lou had in her coat pocket. I had visions of this expanding to its full capacity in the marsh water if it had got wet and thus acting like a sort of airbag to cushion her fall.

We have decided to wait until spring before we venture down to Talley Lakes again.

CHAPTER 14

We had a lovely week with my daughter; she is such easy company and totally undemanding. I think she was blown away by the scenery and the wildlife even at this dreary time of year. Of course the weather wasn't the best but it is January, no doubt she will be back when the weather warms up a bit. Her journey home was uneventful and relatively easy. Miss you already, Lou.

So what has been occurring? Well, due to the weather we were a bit stuck on things to do as a lot of it around here is outdoors. We were going to the Botanic Gardens of Wales primarily to see the butterflies in their butterfly house that breeds tropical species and the like but as there were only two to see this time of year we decided to wait until summer and see all of them.

I had a bit of a fright the other night whilst taking the dogs out. Around here as you can imagine it is pitch black outside as there is no light pollution at all. Part of Trevor's garden runs at the bottom of ours and as I walked toward that end the dogs started barking and growling at something. I stopped to look and saw a figure moving in a high-visibility jacket so I naturally thought it was Trevor.

'Is that you, Trevor?' I said.

No response, but I could see the figure was behind a tree and not answering me. Fearing it was someone perhaps poaching some of his chickens and geese I backed all the way up to the cottage and immediately phoned Trevor and Jill. I was genuinely frightened. Jill answered the phone.

'Hi Jill, it's Hannah, is Trevor there because I have seen a man in your gardens in a high-viz jacket hiding behind a tree.'

'Was he wearing a squirrel hat?' she answered.

'I don't know, it was dark,' I said somewhat bemused.

'It's Trevor,' she said. 'He's gone out to put the geese to bed.'

It suddenly dawned on me that if anyone wanted to break into anywhere they would not be wearing a high-viz jacket and a squirrel hat. I apologised to Jill but I'm not sure she heard me as she was laughing so hard. When I finished the call I turned to see Helen was laughing just as hard.

'But why didn't he answer me?' I said, starting to realise I had been a prize idiot.

A bit later I got an email from Trevor. It read:

'Can't a man have a pee in peace? Sorry I scared you, lots of love and hugs Trevor xxx'

He was peeing behind his tree to leave his male scent and ward off any foxes and predators. I am now very glad it is pitch black out there.

We are going to make a start on the kitchen soon. I tried out the new handles on the doors and it makes so much difference to the units just changing them! I am confident once we have the new worktops and the like the kitchen will be transformed.

We visited a shop just outside Carmarthen this afternoon called 'Charlie's'. It sells everything you can think of. From furniture to greetings cards, pet food to clothes. Name it and Charlie has it. We actually got a huge thrill about being in a 'proper shop'. They had a bit of a sale on too so we nearly wet ourselves with anticipation on entering. But having walked around for a while we left with very little except for some bird food and a couple of greetings cards, however, we enjoyed the experience and plan to go back soon. Helen did grab herself a bargain in the flower planter department and managed to get a large stoneware pot for £20 reduced from £40.

The moon tonight was brilliant. A Super Blue Blood Moon

evidently. It was very bright and lit the garden up, giving it a strange atmospheric feel accompanied by the hooting of the tawny owls. I didn't venture down the end of the garden, not in that light!

I can't believe it has been only eight weeks since we moved here. It does feel like we have been here for absolute ages and I feel have settled in with relative ease. Maybe it's because it is something we wanted for so long it just feels like it was inevitable. Whatever it is, it's made the whole transition from England to Wales very pleasant and so easy.

Yesterday was productive. If you remember we have decided to revamp the kitchen by getting new worktops, removing the existing tiles, giving the Rangemaster oven new door skins from blue to black, changing cupboard handles etc. So I set about seeing how doable it was for us to remove the tiles. Armed with hammer and a chisel tile removing thingy I managed to clear one wall. My OCD was at an all-time high with the mess but all in all I did an OK job. I just have to get the tile adhesive off now and it can be re-plastered. The other wall the tiles are on will not be as easy though, as there are twice as many and in awkward to get at places. Sort of wish I had never started but want the end result. Oh well, onwards and upwards.

We also went in to Llanfwr, running into Jill and Trevor on the way. We all decided to go for a coffee and tea and it made a lovely break to be able to sit back and relax and be waited on. Opposite the pub we were in is Llanfwr's 'Bravissimo' shop. This shop, for the uninitiated, sells ladies' underwear and nightwear. So very sensible and some not so. It's mostly a shop men find themselves in at the last minute on Christmas Eve or their wives or partners' birthdays when they decided to buy a present for her, which will really be for him. We decided after looking in the window to venture in as they had of all things my type of preferred nighties on sale. Trevor and Jill are regular visitors to these premises and I think that is best left there. Anyway the lady in there was a delight. She bristled with enthusiasm and happy as Larry she asked how we knew Trevor and Jill as she had seen us leave the pub with them. We talked about moving here and where we were from. In the end we were there so long and found out so much about her even to the point of looking at all her holiday photos on her tablet. We finally left and once again remarked on how close this community is. I don't mind it at all. Helen isn't so sure, she can't make up her mind if people are just friendly or they are nosy. I think it's just the culture of living a small community.

The afternoon was spent cooking. I made Trevor his Victoria sponge because the look on his little face when I promised him I would make him one was pathetically happy, so it had to be done. I must get my eyes tested and also perhaps my memory because I threw in a tablespoon of baking powder instead of a teaspoon and the sponges when cooked were threatening to break out of the oven and plot world domination. They were massive. Once assembled with jam and fresh cream it looked enormous. I trotted off up the lane in the dark with my trusty head torch and the sponge was well received by all parties. Jill did remark that before moving there I may not have ever considered visiting someone wearing jogging bottoms, rigger boots covered in mud, a coat equally messy with mud and a head torch. I had to laugh about my appearance but she was right, I wouldn't have walked around like that and actually didn't think twice about looking like that. So not only have we embraced this wonderful place but it seems like it has also embraced us.

I look out of the kitchen window and gaze at the surrounding hills. We live in a valley; to the front of the cottage past our garden can be seen the chimneys of the mansion of the estate now laying in disrepair. Evidently someone owns it but chooses not to or can't afford to renovate it. The chimneys still stand proud as if to still impose their eminence of a bygone age as a reminder of their former glory. I would love to just be able to travel back in time to various periods of history, just for a short while as an invisible observer and see life as it was. Not only would it be a complete culture shock but I feel it would be cathartic and would change how we perceive our lives today and how very fortunate we all are regarding all aspects of life, the most prominent being our free healthcare.

Clearly this was a farming estate and the various houses that surround it we have been told were barns and outhouses, now converted into residences. Our cottage started life as a barn and once converted was occupied by a seamstress. I have promised myself that one day I shall take a stroll over to the mansion house and explore the grounds. The only occupants that remain there are barn owls, quite fitting I feel as they are beautiful graceful birds and project their own majesty in flight.

There is so much to explore around here and once the better weather comes I intend to do just that. Roll on spring, nearly there.

St David's Day looms, as does the England vs Wales Six Nations rugby match. Helen and I cannot decide whether to dress up in traditional Welsh costume for St David's or to ignore it like we usually do. I have come to love this country and its people so much I feel quite loyal to Wales, but with that brings guilt about disloyalty to England. As for the rugby, we have decided one of us will cheer for England, the other for Wales.

The leek is one of the national emblems here and I think it's been taken a little too far as we have one in our roof… OK, it's a leak. I may have mentioned before that Wales can be a tad wet. Yesterday the weather excelled itself and it poured all day. On our journey up the stairs to bed I noticed water running down the wall. As my gaze followed the line of water up to the stairwell ceiling it was clear by the bulging plasterboard that something was occurring. I went outside and shining my torch all over that part of the roof I took a guess that the chimney flashing had given up the ghost as all the slate tiles looked intact. We didn't have a choice but to put towels down and pray the rain would stop.

We awoke the next morning to sunshine which was a nice change and the plasterboard had dried out as had the wall. I telephoned Phil. Phil is the guy who is coming to get the tile adhesive off the kitchen walls and to re-plaster. He said he would be round later this morning. In the meantime Trevor popped in for a coffee and took a look around too. He ascertained the loft was OK and the wood up there wasn't affected. He like me also thought it was the flashing around the chimney.

Phil came and started banging on about scaffolding, lifting the chimney, repointing and goodness knows what. By the time he had left we had already decided to get another opinion. Trevor found us someone who is coming in the morning to give his verdict. Let's just hope this one doesn't decide the whole roof needs to come off.

So as you may have gathered we are now at stage two of the kitchen refurbishment. All of the tiles are off. Once the adhesive is done and the walls made good the worktops can be put on and new handles, a bit of paint and Bob's your uncle!

I cannot believe how busy life is in the country. We don't stop. What with the chickens, the garden, the cottage and the minor disasters we are kept occupied most of the day. The chickens are now in full swing egg-laying wise. We had four the other day and usually find them in the afternoon. Hens need daylight to lay eggs and they usually lay six hours after sunrise. One egg we had today was enormous so it looks like they are well established. We are so glad we can lock them away in the dovecote in their house at night as Trevor lost three hens and two cockerels last night due to a male fox. They were in his barn and perched up high so he thinks the fox came in a spooked them and literally knocked them off their perch. As Trevor said with a shrug of his shoulders: 'That's nature for you. Foxes have to eat too.'

I like that philosophy although it must be distressing to find your chickens after the massacre in the morning.

Helen and I watched two kites attempting to catch Trevor's doves today. The white doves flew around in a tight group, moulded to each other, shoulder to shoulder, causing me to coin the phase 'strength in numbers'. The kites called to each other, like two pilots in WW2 Spitfires planning their strategy for a kill in an aerial battle with the Luftwaffe. After much swooping on both sides the kites seemed to give up and literally headed for the hills. The doves, sensing the kites' defeat, went on to give a victory display before returning to Trevor's garden and home.

We actually sat in the garden today at our new cast-iron little table, on our new cast-iron little chairs, and had a cup of tea. I looked across at Helen as she sat there in her mud-splattered coat and trousers with her aptly named muck boots and me in my trappers hat, muddy coat, jogging bottoms and filthy rigger boots looking like some strange white version of Gregory Porter and thought to myself, *You know what? Life doesn't get any better than this.*

CHAPTER 15

It's raining every single day at the moment. The garden resembles a Florida swamp and I wouldn't be at all surprised if we are greeted by an alligator anytime soon when we step into the garden. The dogs get absolutely covered in mud. I looked at them today after they had been playing out for about three hours, thoroughly enjoying themselves until Phoebe, exhausted finally by the fun element of it, wanted her old armchair in the conservatory and a bit of warmth. She actually comes up to me really impatiently trying to get my attention to let her in. So I have to go fill up the large tray by the back door with soapy water and sponge her down to actually reveal her true colour again, and then get her into the conservatory and towel her down before she starts to shake and covers everything in diluted mud. Not always successful but I am getting quicker and pre-empting her every move. Flo, on the other hand, clocks all of this activity and runs for the hills as she hates the 'bath'. The other day in an attempt to get her near me so I could grab her collar I tried chicken, dog biscuits, talking nicely to her, shouting and then cheese. Now cheese is her nemesis, she cannot resist and when I appeared clutching the vintage cheddar I could see the dilemma she now was facing in her eyes. I stood pretending to eat it, making lots of appreciative noises, slurping and totally going over the top. She inched forward and started to make whimpering noises, pathetically crying with longing but knowing what the price of a morsel of this nectar getting in her gob would be. She didn't give in, such was her stubbornness. I did try and rugby tackle her at one point as Helen held her attention to the front of her I sneaked up behind to try the surprise attack from the rear but she must have heard my joints cracking or something as she flew past me, leaving me ending up in a painfully awkward position whilst still standing. I decided not to do that again.

So I have finally cracked this conundrum. All I do is let her in the conservatory covered in mud without the preparatory soapy tray ready. I nonchalantly amble in the door; Phoebe always follows because she has no objection to the warm bath and Flo comes in thinking she has defeated me and knows there's a treat waiting. Then I plan my revenge. In full sight I go into the kitchen, fill up the bucket with soapy water, saunter past her, open the back door and pour it into the tray. On entering the conservatory I grab her collar and et viola! She hates me.

Phoebe today achieved her life-long quest and killed a pheasant. We let her out as usual but unknown to us, a male pheasant had got itself trapped in the space between the henhouse and the fence. She was in there so quickly we didn't stand a chance of saving it. Fortunately it was quick for the bird, but both Helen and I were upset. Phoebe is just following her instincts. Such a powerful fixed pattern of behaviour, nothing could stop it. I picked the bird up and looked at the beautiful feathers and found myself apologising to it. Helen took it up to Trevor as he is no stranger to eating pheasant. He said he would cook it in breadcrumbs and give it to Thomas and tell him it is KFC. Evidently he enjoyed it. I guess it could not have been fresher.

This coming week is busy. Tomorrow, finally, the BT engineer is coming to fix our faulty line. The phone rings once and stops so I have to dial 1471 and ring them back each time as I can never get to the phone on one ring. If it is their fault it's free; if the fault is on our property it's a £129 fee. Sincerely hoping it's them!

Tuesday we have Phil to do the walls in the kitchen, probably a two-day job, we also have Freddie the Fencer coming to finally put the fence up so Phoebe can't get at the side the chickens are on but this is weather dependant so I am not holding my breath on that one, and then Wednesday the man is coming to put new flashing on our chimney. So by the end of the week we are hoping all this is done and we can look forward to the next thing going horribly wrong!

So Phil has arrived and brick dust is drifting its way around the house, getting into every nook and cranny and settling wherever it damn well pleases. I am not a fan. I have tried dusting, wet dusting, vacuuming, sweeping, you name it, I have tried it, but the little pink persistent non-fairy dust wants to stay.

We have Phil in the house at present attending to the plastering of the kitchen walls that had the tiles on them. We hired a hammer chisel in the end to get the tile adhesive off and the wonderful Trevor took over and finished the job, making it look like a knife going through butter. Pleased with the result and not wanting Phil staying here longer than needed we felt it would cut down the cost of his labour significantly.

Phil was due to start Tuesday; first thing we got a phone call saying he would be here at 'tennish'. He arrived at 'elevenish' to tell us he couldn't do anything today as he had an 'emergency' to attend to. Evidently a van laden with scaffolding was wheel deep in mud and he had to help get it out. He then went onto to say very casually that he would probably be here the next day, thinking that two old girls would just accept his flippancy. Helen smiled at him and said in the sweetest of voices, 'Well don't worry, Phil, should you find you can't come tomorrow just give us a phone call first thing and we will find someone else.' I nearly applauded! His face was a picture and I think the penny dropped with him that we were not a pushover.

So he did turn up. Helen and I decided to keep out of his way as he likes to chat and nothing gets done in the meantime, so we stayed in the living room. Every five minutes or so there was a knock on the living room door and every time we were greeted with Phil saying, 'Yeh, there's a bit of a problem.'

Let me give you two examples of these 'problems'.

Problem one.

Phil exclaimed he could not fit an electric box into the gap in the wall to house the unused wires. He said there were bits of wall preventing it. Helen took a hammer and chisel and tapped it gently and they came off. She handed the tools back to him and exited.

Problem two.

Phil exclaimed he could not get a screw out of the other socket in the wall. I stood there and looked and took the screwdriver off him and turned it without effort. I walked away, puzzled.

At the end of the day he said he was pleased with his preparations and will do the plastering tomorrow. I sincerely hope so before we both go into meltdown.

So later tonight the stonemason came to measure the kitchen for the granite worktops. I felt sorry for him as he had driven from Manchester and arrived in the dark at Talley and got completely lost. After trying to get him here I went out and found him about a mile away. The sat navs do not recognise our postcode too well and in the dark I couldn't tell him any landmarks to look out for. Actually when I say landmarks I use the term very loosely, what I mean is the broken farm gate, the sign by the side of the road hanging by one screw and the large puddle that goes halfway across the road. Significant features around here.

So we are hoping after tomorrow the kitchen will be ready to paint over the weekend and then next week we have to remove the worktops and unplumb the taps and sink on the Wednesday before the fitter arrives. Can't wait!

We also have a chap coming Friday evening to measure up the three windows for shutters, so our kitchen refurbishment is well underway. I just hope it looks like we both image when it's done, but we have worked out that the kitchen will get a completely new look for a fraction of the cost of a whole new kitchen so it can be done!

Yesterday being Pancake Day, we asked Jill and Trevor to come for a pancake feast with the kids in tow. We had a lovely evening, all sitting around the table while Helen worked her pancake magic and cooked in all twenty pancakes served with lemons and sugar or Nutella (yuck) or golden syrup.

On Monday afternoon while the sun was shining we put my mum's ashes in a container, a blue one as it was her favourite colour, and planted a rose called 'Mum in a Million'. It's a pink fragrant rose and I look forward to seeing it in the summer when it becomes established. I will take the container with me wherever I go if I ever do move, so she will always be with me, but then again she is anyway. Grief is a strange emotion. Some days I feel so desperately sad and the slightest thing can make me emotional and other days I can be quite pragmatic and know she had a good life and it was her time. Because she was ninety-eight both my sister Pat and I were pulled almost into this sense of 'she will always be here'. In fact I think the grandchildren did also. Mum was there and that was that. When she went it was a shock almost because of this false sense of security we had been lulled into. The whole thing was made worse by the nature of her passing too. We all took it for granted she would go in her sleep, not because of a fall she could not recover from. Whichever way you wrap this up, losing someone, whatever their age or however they go, will punch you in the gut and wind you for a very long time. I haven't even started to get my breath back yet.

CHAPTER 16

It seems today we had the most powerful earthquake, measuring 4.4 on the Richter scale, for a decade in the UK and the worst since 1906 in Wales. Helen and I had spent a few hours at Llandysuls Gardening Weekend and then at the Farmyard Nurseries and were happily on our way home when it happened. We didn't feel a thing and had no idea until we stopped at our local pub to get some butter (it acts as a shop and post office too). The landlady who was a Jo Brand lookalike asked us if we had felt it as she said she had nearly fallen off her chair. We looked at each other in bewilderment and checked our phones to make sure it wasn't April 1st. However, once we got home our neighbour Mary informed us she nearly fell off her chair too such was the tremor it produced. She said there was no noise, just the movement. So the one and only time we experience an earthquake neither of us knew! My daughter-in-law informed me later that she heard a lady in a Swansea pub being interviewed post-earthquake who thought it was just someone slamming a door and that was the epicentre!

Llandysul Gardening Weekend was lovely. Nearby is Farmyard Nursery, owned by a lovely chap who actually won a gold in the Chelsea Flower Show for his hellebores. It is vast and you would need a day to really absorb all it has to offer. I managed to get a Myrtle plant. The flower it produces is a beautiful, white, delicate flower which has been used in royal wedding bouquets since Queen

Victoria's daughter's wedding in 1858. I love the delicate flowers of this plant and Helen and I walked away with a few free plants given to us courtesy of the owner.

We have had such a busy week. The plastering is now all done and we must admit to being pleased with the finished result, so the two and a half days with Phil was worth suffering. The fencing has started to go up and should be done Monday so Phoebe can no longer get at the chickens and can run free in the garden without traumatising the birds.

Tomorrow we have to lightly rub down the new plaster and start painting. I will be so glad when this is finished.

Next week Carol and Steve will be here to help us and Steve is putting up the greenhouse for us so we can start with our veggie growing! We are also having an area of land rotovated to provide a good area of soil to plant potatoes and brassicas.

It finally looks like spring could be approaching. It's staying lighter, feeling slightly warmer and the new shoots pushing their way through our garden borders give us a glimmer of hope that things will look a bit greener out there soon.

At the moment I am desperately trying to find a plumber who can plumb in the new sink and attach the new taps Tuesday afternoon so we can have the water back on again. Fingers crossed 'Local Hero', 'Check a Trade' etc. will find us someone. It's that or the four of us will have to go a long time without a wash, a cup of tea or God forbid be able to use the loo!

Carol and Steve arrived on Monday in the midst of us halfway through trying to get the newly plastered walls sanded down and painted. We pulled off the old pelmets circa 1960 and the cobwebs and dead flies that came with them were, I think, from the Jurassic period. Taking these things of beauty off the walls resulted in gaps in the old plaster which then had to be Polyfilled. We worked like stink and managed to get most of it done in time for the worktops to turn up the next day.

Steve is putting up our greenhouse for us but in addition to that he is changing our light sockets and switches, the cupboard door handles and today got the old worktops and sink ready for the next day. All this after driving five hours to get here. We are truly blessed with these two.

So the next day the worktop fitters were due to arrive between 8 and 10am. They actually turned up on the doorstep at 7:30 having left West London at 03:45am. One of them was very young and I wondered if he was working during half-term week! I made them some tea and Helen did some toast as they were waiting for the actual granite to turn up. The young boy sat at our table helping himself to toast and marmalade and looked very comfortable and through a mouth full of food mumbled, 'No-one has ever given me breakfast before.'

Once the granite arrived they set about cutting and trimming and making a bloody mess and noise. In addition to this Fred the Fencer turned up to tell us he wasn't coming. At one point Helen had trod in dog poo in the garden and unbeknown to her trailed it across their dust sheets. Frantically trying to get rid of the evidence she got out the antibacterial wipes and was in the middle of cleaning up when the young lad came in, sniffed and said, 'Granite don't arf smell when it's cut, don't it?'

The day proceeded with the stonemason discovering that the window sill replacements we ordered had not been measured correctly and so we have to wait for them to be delivered so I can place them myself. Paul the mason showed me how so hopefully I can do it. It is relatively simple. They finally finished and the plumber turned up as arranged and we are so pleased with it all. We are also relieved we did not decide to get new cabinets. Just changing the handles, refreshing the paintwork and replacing the tired old worktops has transformed it and it looks like a new kitchen.

Things are starting to come together nicely. The roof is fixed, the kitchen is all but complete. The greenhouse is under construction so seeds can start to be sown. The much-needed fence is almost done so the dogs cannot get to the chickens and they have loads of room now to run around freely and play. As Carol pointed out, maybe it was fortunate we moved in the winter as all the jobs have been done in bad weather and once spring and summer arrive we can dedicate our time to the garden. There is so much to do out there!

Helen, Carol and I all went into Lampeter today after showing Carol the delights of the municipal dump where we got rid of yet more mountains of rubble, cardboard and general rubbish. Lampeter is a university town full of chic coffee shops, vegetarian restaurants and younger residents or visitors are dressed in very boho/hippie attire. I quite liked the whole laid-back environment. We had lunch in one of the vegetarian restaurants and the food was amazing. One of the main fixations I had today was to buy peanut butter for the birds. They love it and at 69p a large jar, if you get the basic brand, is a low-cost way of helping the birds much-needed fat store for the colder nights ahead. I asked Carol to remind me to get some when we got to Sainsbury's.

Walking along back to the car on our way to Sainsbury's I asked her what it was I asked her to remind me to get, at which point she confessed she could not remember. I duly turned to Helen to see if she had picked up a snippet of conversation regarding the required item and she had less idea than we did. Fortunately it did come to me and my fixation was satiated. The running joke all the way around the shop was based on the peanut butter theme and became hysterically funny. The three of us out together should be supervised. None of us had the shared brain cell today and leaving us to wander aimlessly through the streets of Lampeter is not a good idea. It was a lovely day.

Tomorrow the four of us are having a day at home. Carol is making us some covers for the arms of our new sofas before Flo and Phoebe scratch it to an unrecognisable state in their efforts to bark at anything that moves or doesn't move in the garden. I am going to finish the unfinished in the kitchen, Steve is building the greenhouse and Helen has about a million and one plants to sow, plant or generally find a home for.

Roll on tomorrow, this is fun now!

After a lovely week, Steve finished the greenhouse which looks amazing, changed all our kitchen sockets and light switches and about another hundred things. Carol helped prepare dinners and made my sofa arm covers to stop the dogs desecrating the new leather. They are pretty special people. Friends like these do not come along very often and we treasure them. They are home safe and sound now.

Last night we all went to Colbran Inn, strangely enough in a village called Colbran! The inn has been in existence for about three hundred years. Colbran is a tiny village and the rooms in this pub are tiny to match. The pub is at the centre of the village and is run by the community. It is also a post office and shop again run by the community. Every Saturday night people take turns to cook. There are seventeen places, so booking is a must and it is always fully booked. The menu caters for both vegetarians and meat eaters and the food was amazing. What a lovely experience the whole thing was and a tribute to what can be done when a community comes together for a common cause. The bar was about twelve feet square and the actual dining room about fourteen by twenty feet. I still work in old measurements, nothing else makes any sense to me so apologies to the new metric generation, for once if you are reading this you will have to look up a conversion chart like I do all the time.

We waved goodbye to our dear friends this morning and spent the day in the garden. Now we finally have the fence up we can let the dogs run around unsupervised, although Phoebe still tries her escapology tricks and today I found her staring at a small gap in the wire fence that overlooks the bottom of the stream and I could tell she was contemplating how on earth she was going to squeeze through it to terrorise the chickens. Her efforts were foiled by one look from me in her direction. She almost pretended to be sniffing something interesting in that area, trying to kid me she had no interest whatsoever in the fence and the minuscule hole that lay between her and her carnivorous longing.

The weather for the whole week has been amazingly beautiful. It really has given us a snapshot of how our summer will evolve and the days are now becoming longer. New shoots are pushing their way through the frozen earth only to find a hostile welcome from the frost. I don't think I have ever seen a frost like these ones. The ground is like concrete and I can watch the sun moving around the garden melting it in its wake, leaving white shadows where it can't reach. The garden birds are desperate for food. Their favourite is the peanut butter pine cone feeder and also I decided to smear some on the tree, but Helen has told me off, telling me it looked like a peanut butter tree and she is sure it is not good for it. Still trying to work out why. Steve had a first while he was here, he saw a great spotted woodpecker from the kitchen window. I was so pleased for him. I love it when people see a 'first' in wildlife. We sometimes have four woodpeckers all vying for a chomp at the fat ball feeders. They can get quite nasty with each other and it's handbags at dawn some days. The most abundant of our garden birds are the tits – marsh, great, blue, longtailed and coal. I know Helen and I are wildlife nerds but at least we are nerds together.

We can really feel things coming together now. The greenhouse, the kitchen, the bathroom and Helen is working so hard in the garden. She has planted out the orchard, has started to plant out hawthorn hedging, twenty-two plants in all. Hopefully these will attract even more birds and screen our garden nicely to give it a bit of a respite from the winter winds that blow in down the valley. The better weather does cheer you up no end, however, as I am sure everyone is aware a big freeze is on its way. With a wind-chill factor evidently Wednesday here will be -5°C. So as my dear old mum always said to me, even in the height of summer, 'Make sure you wear your vest.'

CHAPTER 17

Well the much-heralded Beast from the East has certainly arrived although not so much in snowfall but definitely dropping the temperature to sub-zero. There are three polar bears chasing seals in our garden.

Our chickens do not like this weather. The minute I open their coop to let them out into their pen they fly out with anticipation and almost fly back in again. The only thing that keeps them out is the much-needed food and they are addicted to warmed spaghetti, a feeding tip given to me by a friend. They go mad for it, almost mobbing me as I approach with the container of steaming faux worms. Happy hens and loads of eggs, so many I am now giving them away to neighbours and people I pass in the street. I wish Jeremy Hunt would visit so I could chuck some at him.

Helen has gone away for a funeral so I am here alone with the dogs and hens. How she got to Eastbourne I will never know, driving through a blizzard at one point. She is catching up with her friends at her old place of work and then going up to Croydon Friday. En route she will see Carol and Steve; although the visit was planned before it is even more poignant now as they lost their beloved dog Charlie, suddenly and without any warning. He was only seven years old and the sweetest boy, completely bonkers as all boxers are and just loved people. He had a wonderful life with them but their loss is palpable.

RIP, lovely boy. It's been a bad week regarding the loss of dogs; my cousin lost hers on Monday and I read with sadness another friend had to say goodbye to hers. Our pets are not just animals to us owners, they are family members and the love we feel for them is as real and tangible as love we feel for any other member of our family.

So what shall I do without Helen's supervision? This morning I am going to show Jill how to sell on eBay as she has a knackered Smart Car she wants rid of for parts only. I may go for a quick dip in the river and take in some rays in the back garden. Either that or light a log fire and wrap up warm and go out as little as possible. I can hear as I type, the wind whipping up outside and the snowflakes are swirling outside the bedroom window. I feel like I am in one of those glass paper weights with the false snow scenes and someone keeps shaking it… a lot!

The snow brings with it a certain stillness which I must confess I quite like. It's almost as if Mother Nature has called a halt to all the mayhem and business that the human race feels it must commit to and just lets us breathe peacefully for a moment in time. Everything slows down. However, here in this part of Wales nothing had to stop, it never really started.

I watched a party political broadcast for Plaid Cymru last night and was very impressed. I also felt the new artwork 'There but not there' in memory of the WW1 lost that will be appearing throughout the country was quite inspired and almost ghost-like, which of course I think it is meant to be. The metalwork ones of the lost miners are especially moving. I always feel such sadness as I too lost family in both wars and their sacrifice should never be forgotten; one only has to read the works of the WW1 poets like Wilfred Owen and Siegfried Sassoon to be propelled into the hell that for them was every day and every part of their existence. My particular favourite WW1 poem is 'Naming of Parts' by Henry Reed. In this he juxtapositions the nature around him with the lessons he is having to attend to learn how to use a gun. If you don't know it, do read it, it is simply genius.

Although I am quite happy with my own company and never get bored, Ty Mawr is not the same without Helen around. I guess the timing of her visit weather-wise could have worked out better as the conditions here have been difficult.

The wind that came up from the valley thanks to Storm Emma

has been fierce. I stepped outside yesterday when it was at its peak and could barely hold the door back from slamming, throwing me into it as I lost my footing in the snow and ice that has built up over the last few days. The greenhouse suffered in the wind and we lost eight panes of glass at the back end where it took the full force of the wind. It looks pretty though!

The garden birds are really struggling and I managed to get ten large jars of peanut butter delivered before all deliveries here ceased due to the road conditions. They birds love it. This morning I put out a whole jar for them, smearing it onto different branches and bird feeders and stones on the ground so both ground feeders and small birds could feast on the much-needed fat it provides.

Such a treat to see them in their frenzied quest to store fat to survive. If you don't feed the birds, please do.

Yesterday saw a lapwing make an appearance in the garden. At this time of year in these conditions, all sorts of unexpected garden visitors will turn up to get some food. I thought I had a firecrest also but a very clever friend of mine has identified it for me and it is the goldcrest. I live in hope. The goldcrest usually such a shy little bird was on our bridge that crosses our stream frantically searching for fat morsels dropped by the overhead feeders. I was within two feet of it and it still stayed there such was its hunger. What a treat that was!

Another little visitor was found amongst the chicken feed and it was a field vole. I had never seen one up close before and managed to catch it and set it free from the large green plastic box it couldn't scramble up the sides of. I had a really close look whilst it was in my hand and it is so tiny with its little round head and almost imperceptible ears. I feel so lucky being this close to all sorts of nature. The spring and summer no doubt will bring more treats with them. The previous owners informed us there is a resident common lizard amongst the undergrowth near the vegetable patch so I am looking forward to being able to get some shots of that; both Helen and I are keen amateur photographers and have been fortunate enough to win a few small prizes with our photographs, all of wildlife and nature.

Trevor and Jill have been lovely as usual while Helen has been away. Poor Trevor yesterday was despatched by me off to the GP as they asked me to look at his eye following having a piece of sawdust fly into it whilst sawing logs. The sight that greeting me was a very red swollen eye, swollen cheek and red forehead. Orbital cellulitis! He now has the right antibiotics but moaned and said all he wanted me to do was pull out his eyelid and scrape the sawdust out with a cotton bud! I declined.

He phones me every night to make sure I am warm and to advise me on the best way to stay alive during the night and I reassure him I am still alive and kicking and still able to get around unaided. I am older than his mother would have been had she lived, so I must seem like a frail old pensioner to him. It makes me laugh but joking apart, Trevor would go to the ends of the earth to make sure we are OK. Special man.

So another day looms. Hopefully tomorrow Helen will be back with our friend Jane in tow. She is staying for a week and celebrating Helen's 60th with us. Quite a milestone. Helen is not sure what she wants to do on the day and it all depends on the weather etc. so watch this space.

CHAPTER 18

During the Beast from the East cold snap, and I mean COLD, something happened to the connection to our cottage. BT do not know what and it goes without saying we are clueless. All we know is we have no phone or internet. That's all we know. So I telephone on my mobile of course and inform them, explaining after having to go through all the button pressing for about an hour and a half.

'Please press one if you are phoning from the telephone that has a fault.'

'Please press two if you are phoning about the fault and your phone is working.'

'Please press three if you are ringing from the phone that isn't working.'

'Please press four if you think our questions are ridiculously stupid.'

I pressed four…

So I speak to someone human at last and go through security yet again even though I have just gone through it with a recorded voice and explain the problems I am having.

Q. 'Is your phone working?'

A. 'No, that is why I am phoning you from my mobile.'

Q. 'Have you a dial tone?'

A. 'No, the phone is not working.'

Q. 'I will just test your line, are you OK to hold?'

A. 'Yes.'

A further five minutes go past with me listening to music on a loop.

He is back… 'Thank you for holding, your phone is not working.'

Anyway, this went on for another half a decade and then finally it was established that our phone line was not working and that we would need an engineer to visit the box that is about half a mile from here to sort it out. We should be up and running in two days, he assured me. So with a resolute sigh I thanked him and hung up.

Three days later still without a dial tone and suspecting, based this time on reliable information, that our phone wasn't working:

'Please press one if you are suicidal due to our incompetence.' Etc., etc…

I pressed one.

They informed me my phone line was still not working and their engineers were trying to locate the fault, but the latest update from the engineer assures us the fault should be fixed in two days.

I started to lose confidence for some reason, call me a pessimist.

So stupidly in the said two days I rang again.

'Please press one if you are devoid of any will to live.'

I pressed one.

I was informed that BT were devastated to hear that my phone was not working for so long and that the fault will be fixed on Monday 12th at the latest at 16:25 hours. Honestly, I kid you not. If after this magical, mystical, bewitching hour we still don't have a phone line our fault will be escalated to urgent. I played the pensioner card, yes you read right, for the first time in my life I found myself saying, 'I live in deepest, darkest Wales and I am a pensioner, I need this phone line.' Pathetic.

It will make no difference because now BT have me down as a daft old bag who probably can't use the internet anyway.

Talk about shoot yourself in the foot.

So as promised BT did come through, although I think it may have been ever so slightly pushed along by me spotting the BT van up the road as I drove Helen back from the dentist and pursued him, which entailed me climbing up a bank where he was fiddling around with a square box and lots of wires. After having explained who I was, i.e. a victim, he promised me I would be the first to be mended and he would phone me when I was reunited with the 21st century. And he did! Within ten minutes of getting indoors the phone rang and voila! Returned to full function. Bless his little grubby socks.

During the BT famine we also encountered a four and a half hour loss of electricity which was fun. Luckily as we have a log burner and a Calor gas cooker we were able to eat and keep warm, however, we ended up with Trevor and Jill as they were without power also and we all gathered around their fire in candlelight chatting and laughing and remarking on how without music, TV and the internet we can just about survive.

Helen had a tooth out today and it was no breeze! Now Helen has no fear of the dentist. Hang on, I shall rephrase that; Helen used to have no fear of the dentist. This was a bottom molar that was on its way out to tooth nirvana. So I dropped her off at the dentist at 11 o'clock and walked to the bakery and the bank. Just to explain, this takes about ten minutes. On the way back to the car I took a detour and got some bottled water for Helen; all in all the whole thing took twenty minutes tops. I arrived at the dentist's and just as I got inside the door my mobile rang with Helen's ringtone and she was at the car! When I reached her she was white and shaking and it was clear she had been on the end of a less-than-pleasant experience. Given the time lapse there was no way in the world the mepivacaine used as a numbing agent had been given sufficient time to work so consequently Helen felt the whole thing. She said at one point the dentist pulled so hard, her knees came up with the pain. Anyone who knows Helen knows she is strong and stoic, so if she says it hurt it really hurt. The dentist told her not to drink alcohol for twenty-four hours so she opened up some scotch when she got in and knocked back a couple of glasses, declaring the pain subsided. With the painkillers and alcohol she spent a very happy if not floaty afternoon in the garden watching pink elephants and little pixies frolicking around the vegetable patch. I on the other hand repaired the damage Storm Emma had caused to the greenhouse, deciding I was better served using Perspex instead of horticultural glass as replacements. I managed to cut it to size and fit all the panes back to where they should be. Horticultural glass for the uninitiated and uninterested amongst you has the consistency of thin ice. Even a hard stare could shatter it into pieces. I have a feeling as more glass gives way to the elements or the dogs the Perspex will be the material of choice.

The hens have wreaked havoc on their little patch of grass outside the dovecote. It has turned into the consistency of the bottom of a very old neglected pond with a smell to match. On one of my many trips into the pen to shovel the proverbial chicken shit I am faced with three muddy, manic chickens almost fleecing me now for spaghetti. Every time I make an appearance near tIem the noise they make becomes almost deafening. They love pasta! I swear their clucking has taken on a slight Italian accent and Edna wants to open up a restaurant and go to the opera.

The eggs keep coming and coming and coming. I have tried to get my neighbour, the eminent Professor David, to come off his low-cholesterol diet and lighten our egg load and he resisted until yesterday when he spotted me knee deep in the chicken swamp clutching (no pun intended) three eggs. He declared he was going to have a fry-up and they would go very nicely with it. I just told him to double up on his statins and enjoy.

We had Jane here last week, Helen's long-standing friend. They were eight when they met at school and have been firm friends ever since. Jane was enamoured with our cottage and lifestyle and it was lovely that she was here for Helen's birthday. We all went out for a really lovely meal at the Cawdor Hotel in Llanfwr and I have now tasted the most sumptuous, amazing, orgasmic ice cream ever made. Homemade clotted cream flavour. I'll just leave that there. Suffice to say I will return.

*

I was just stepping out of the shower this morning and Helen walked past to go into another bedroom. She glanced in my direction and about one minute later I heard her singing that most romantic of songs 'Hey Fatty Boom Boom'. She swears it was totally unintentional but I have a strong suspicion the melody was psychologically triggered. Bugger that clotted cream ice cream.

I have finally fixed the windswept greenhouse and am hoping that all Steve's hard work will not get battered by any more storms. I spent most of the day in there sowing seeds for this year and boy, was it hot. I stopped and looked around me to take in all the sights and sounds of my surroundings. The hills lay in front of me and the sound of spring lambs echoed down the valley. Kites and buzzards flew overhead, the kites with their high-pitched whistle and the mewing sound of the buzzards interjected the buzzing of the newly risen bees and other insects. The birds were amazingly active; this is their time, they are so busy finding a mate, preparing nests for the spring clutches they hope to have. In the dovecote a robin has decided it would be a great place to bring up her family and I find all sorts of moss and straw laying around on top of the chicken house left in her wake and eagerness to build her home. In addition to the wildlife I have the gentle bubbling of the flowing stream right beside me and the gush of the river competing in an ambient sound contest with the stream. I find myself sighing often, even tearful at times. I walked around the garden where Helen was rearranging plants and digging up small trees and generally clearing areas to create her up and coming projects. She has such vision and although this is going to be hard work as the garden area is huge, she will do it and it's going to look wonderful. Arches and water features, wooded areas and irises galore. I picked some of the daffodils that the dogs had mashed into the ground and salvaged what I could. One I laid on my mum's rose planter just to let her know she was part of it all.

My next project is to turn a large piece of lawn into a vegetable bed. All the wood was delivered today from our local builders' yard. Every time I go in there I get odd looks but I suppose it's not every day a sixty-four-year-old woman rocks up in rigger boots, dirty trousers, muddy coat and hair piled on top of her head looking completely insane. It wasn't until I left I realised I had two pairs of glasses on my head and sunglasses on my face. If someone had told me twenty years ago I would be walking around like this, covered in mud and resembling something out of the 'Thriller' video I would have probably believed them to be honest. I have always been slightly odd. They take pity on me in there and humour me to the best of their ability. It's one of those places that if you ask for something it is either tucked away at the back, under the counter or stored 'out back'. I am so tempted to ask for fork handles.

The dogs are having the time of their lives. All day long they run around the garden playing. Neither of them are interested in the usual doggy pursuits like a ball or a stick. These two just play together. Phoebe stops now and again to terrorise the birds or thinks she has heard something very suspicious and has to run to it with haste only to find absolutely nothing occurring. Flo looks on in bewilderment as she has no idea what is going on. Flo's sole purpose in life is to have fun at any cost and anything that remotely resembles being canine is alien to her. Phoebe knows she is a dog and acts like one. Flo doesn't know what she is. Come to that, both Helen and I are puzzled on that one too. Now and again Flo appears to get the gist of this dog thing and will sniff enthusiastically at something but she soon loses interest and carries on looking silly but happy. A bit like us, really.

Helen's gum was still very sore and painful but today she left off the alcohol and made do with painkillers instead. By the end of the day it was feeling slightly better. She has to have a softish diet so I made a quiche so I could use up at least some of the mountain of eggs we have. Any future visitors will be going home with eggs, so be warned. I have purchased egg boxes so this is serious. Remember when I was moaning they hadn't produced? I think the old adage of 'be careful what you wish for' is very apt, don't you?

CHAPTER 19

The past week has been busy. My plans for the vegetable area are coming to fruition now. With the help of Trevor and Jill, Helen and I have built two vegetable beds measuring thirty feet by nine feet and one is now full with compost, some from the existing compost heap we acquired and some from the vast amount we had delivered. We have enough compost to help out Kew Gardens if they run out; let's hope it does its job and our veggies are edible at least.

Unfortunately Monday night I had a dreadful bout of sinusitis which drove me to the GP for some antibiotics and glad to report they are working and my face ache has gone… even though I still get called it frequently.

We have come to the conclusion that mud is an essential part of living here. It is no longer a question of 'do I have mud on my clothes?' It is more 'how much mud do I have on my clothes?' So we spend half our time in muddy clothes and the other half in our pyjamas. The dream of sitting in the garden sipping something cool on one of the many seating areas has in reality become the place we crawl to at the end of the day and collapse. We have so much to do and just as we feel spring is on its way, the weather turns and we are all up to our necks in snow. Spring will happen but maybe not yet.

We woke up this morning with a fairly thick covering of snow. Poor Helen after having a tooth extracted by a medieval torturer on

Monday has now got a toothache on the other side of her mouth and what looks like to me, with the use of my otoscope, like another start of an ear infection. She barely slept with it and when I came downstairs this morning a bottle of scotch was on the kitchen table where she had desperately tried to hold the alcohol on her tooth to numb the pain. I could see she was in agony and this stayed all day until this evening when she said it has subsided a bit. GP first thing in the morning for the ear and hopefully the antibiotics she has for that will sort out the tooth.

So far the phone line has been working three days without failing which must be some sort of record for here. BT have sent me a phone bill for £171 which includes £126 for fixing the phone. I will be having a little chat with them tomorrow.

I am hoping that all the seedlings I sowed in the greenhouse have not been killed off by the mini Beast from the East. Our poor daffodils look knackered with a capital F.

One of the chickens has become broody. It's Gertie. She sits on her nest all day and will not eat or drink unless I physically turf her off the nest. She has stopped laying eggs and has commandeered Edna and Gladys's eggs. Those two at the moment, they couldn't care less about having kids and would rather go clubbing, drink wine and misbehave. I tried to lift Gertie off the nest the other day and boy did she go for me! I was so pleased I was wearing gardening gloves! Today I attempted to get her off and I thought someone had superglued her bum to the straw. She would not shift. The problem is she is in great danger of starving herself to death and also on making the other two become like her. We have to take the eggs out as soon as possible so she gets the idea she could not be with chick! She has even plucked out some chest feathers to line the nest. I am so glad we don't have to pluck anything out when we are pregnant apart from our eyebrows as an option.

The eggs when you eventually get at them are so warm it is incredible. I put one in my trouser pocket and could literally feel the warmth through the material. I feel so sorry for her; she clearly would make an excellent Mother Hen. I asked Trevor and Jill if they wanted her for brooding and they are now trying to get us to mate her and raise chicks. Trevor said we could borrow his rabbit hutch to put her in away from the others but I am afraid the chicks will get confused and start eating carrots and hopping everywhere. We will see; it wasn't in our plans to have chicks or even confused bunnies but who knows? Anything here is possible.

So back to the tooth and ear problem. At this point I have to explain that even though she was a health professional, she is the most resistant person I know to sort out her own problems health wise, therefore, instead of phoning the GP she decided to see if it would settle down which resulted in her literally being awake all night in intractable pain.. Thankfully she did get an appointment Tuesday and in the dentist's words has a 'raging infection' in three parts of her tooth and gum. So she is on antibiotics and so far not a lot of change, although she said she feels slightly improved.

We had a lovely surprise when Trevor phoned to invite us up to his to see the twin lambs born to one of his ewes, both beautiful little creatures and as sweet as anything apart from their smell! However, within hours one of them died. It transpires that the ewe just did not possess any maternal instincts and hasn't produced enough milk to feed them. The remaining lamb is now firmly ensconced in Trevor's house, running around the kitchen and being bottle fed. Helen gave a feed this afternoon and is smitten; her maternal instincts only arise when there is a baby animal. Give her a baby human and she makes all the right noises but you can tell she is looking for the next cooing woman to hand it to.

The weather is cold, literally freezing. I got up this morning to a really heavy frost and fog. The surrounding grounds looked like a frozen white mass resembling Antarctica and even the dogs make no impression on the frigid grass when they trample across it in their haste to have their first wee and sniff out whatever dared to come into their territory during the night. I know we have a visiting fox as Phoebe spends a long time on her back rolling in its poo and I spend a long time washing her back to get rid of the rancid odour. As I crunched along the lawn I could hear a tawny owl who had obviously set its clock to the wrong time or had been out clubbing and was late home; this coupled with the fog and the silence cast an eerie atmosphere in the garden. Everything seemed momentarily frozen in time until my reverie was shattered by Flo and Phoebe taking off on their leads in pursuit of a female pheasant and forgetting I was on the other end of it all.

We are so busy. The old saying about when retired you wonder how you ever fitted in work is so true. One of our current jobs is siting our table and chairs to one side of the garden where another part of the stream flows by the side and we can hear the water running constantly; it gives the gentle sound of a babbling brook which we are hoping will lend to the whole ambience of dining outside, however, knowing our luck it will just make us both have to run to the loo as running water does it to me every time. We are also helping Trevor and Jill remove the ivy from their walls. The walls are beautiful but unfortunately the ivy has become so overgrown the wall is starting to suffer. It's a phenomenally huge task but we are giving them a couple of hours every afternoon to help them along. They have certainly done enough for us.

We are off the Carmarthen tomorrow to see some real shops. We are both excited about going to Aldi's... This demonstrates the depths of desperation for retail therapy; we feel like we have been living like survivors from a nuclear holocaust. Not that there is anything wrong with Aldi's, quite the contrary, but to be excited about visiting it is really quite tragic. We are also going to Charlie's, the shop that sells everything from jubilee clips to knickers. I guess shops are so rare they stock everything so all can be acquired in one hit. Last time we were there we bought bird food, a fleece jumper, a doily and some wooden crates. Embrace diversity, I say.

Helen's tooth pain started to get a little better day by day but only really gave her some respite after five days. She has suffered and toothache as I am sure you will agree is a vile pain.

So, onwards and upwards. We spent the week in and out of the garden. We always have something to do here and it's usually major construction works rather than tinkering pleasantly, idling away the hours. This week we have hung all our pictures at long last, installed a rainwater barrel on the greenhouse, built staging for the greenhouse, put together a bathroom cabinet, made a bed for fruit bushes and planted blackberries, gooseberries and raspberries. Also planted out shallots, garlic and sown every vegetable seed you can think of. Helen has dug borders, planted out different plants, sawn things, moved things and planned some amazing projects for the garden involving roses. In addition to all of this the shopping, housework and cooking had to be done. I have worked out why a lot of farmhouses are knackered-looking and my theory is the family, if they are farming, are too tired to do anything indoors or have no time to.

Our trip to Aldi and Charlie's proved to be disappointing on the whole as Aldi's had just reopened after a refurbishment, which means they have made the aisles even narrower so everyone has to walk like a crab with a trolley, all in a frantic manner and to be honest I did a bit of people watching and no-one looked happy. They all looked like they were fed up with walking like crabs with trolleys. So we scuttled our way around there with everyone else and then after, paid a visit to Charlie's where you get lulled into that false sense of everything being a bargain. I actually was very good and restricted myself to only things I needed whereas Helen, starved of her retail therapy fixes made a few unnecessary purchases. It's not everyone who can wear a high-viz jacket and Helen is not one of them. I saw her walking around in one in search of a mirror. I thought she looked like a lollipop lady and thankfully she must have found the mirror as it did not end up in her trolley. However, two new mugs to join the other twenty-seven we possess, one pair of utility trousers made with material the consistency of cardboard, two pairs of gardening gloves to add to the nineteen pairs we have, a pair of waterproof trousers and several other equally surplus to requirements items later we advanced to the checkout. She did look happy until she got to the checkout and then her face did alter slightly; gone was the manic grin and it was replaced by a sort of lopsided grimace. I thought she was having a stroke at first until it dawned on me she was suffering from being 'Charlied'. *Kerching!*

So the clocks sprang forward and this morning the promise of summertime advancing was evident. I got up at the new hour of eight o'clock fully aware it was really seven o'clock and feeling disgruntled. However, my mood lifted when I saw the sunshine streaming through the bedroom window and then on venturing out into the garden with the dogs for their morning ablutions it hit me full in the face. The sun was the brightest I have ever seen it here; overhead the sky, a jigsaw-puzzle blue stretched beyond and over the valley and the vivid green of the hills were dotted with little cotton wool balls of braying sheep and lambs that echoed in the stillness of the morning. Bees were buzzing, flies were flying and the cacophony of birdsong was almost deafening as I walked around our garden. Even the dogs seemed to sense the beauty of it all and walked slowly as if in respect of the dawning of the summertime and all that nature has to give. So many people said to us that if we like it here in the winter, we will love it in the summer. They were not wrong.

CHAPTER 20

I spent the first part of the week suffering from the after-effects of the methotrexate drug I inject weekly. It's a horrible feeling and makes me exhausted, to the point where I can hardly get out of bed, which makes me feel depressed because there is so much I want to do. So once again I have decided to finish taking it for good and look at alternatives. Enough is enough.

Anyway, onwards and upwards, the latter part of the week has been so much better. The weather has been changeable but on the whole you can tell summer is trying its best to warm us all up and stir the ground into producing new shoots, and the daffodils around Ty Mawr are abundant. We had the snowdrops a few weeks back which were profuse and now the white blanket has been replaced by a bobbing yellow wave of happy-looking flowers. No wonder Wordsworth waxed lyrical about them.

The chickens are acting very oddly. Gertie's insistence on becoming a mother has spilled over to Gladys and Edna, although Edna is less affected to be honest. She has attitude with a capital A. So now we have had to lock Gertie out of the hut until bedtime otherwise she doesn't move or eat and drink. She looked really cross to begin with and at one point charged towards me as I went to leave. I swear she stuck her chest out and huffed at me. However, it appears to be working keeping them in the pen all day with no chance of escape. They do go into the dovecote (no longer appropriately named, I feel) and perch on the beams of wood we have placed, crisscrossing the interior, so they are not exposed to the elements. So we will have to see how they fare. Evidently according to Trevor about a week should do it.

We have just registered with the Welsh Water Board as we forgot! After receiving a letter threatening to cut off the water as the property appeared empty I informed them of our presence and we received a bill from them for the time we have been here and the next year in total. It is so cheap! Given the fact we have no waste water as we have the soak away it's still very cheap, working out to £16 per month. We figured it is because there is so much of it! So every black cloud and all that. Sorry, could not resist.

We are enjoying the garden and the vegetables are all sown now. The greenhouse is a sanctuary. I sit in there sowing my seeds with my phone playing music or videos of my choice. It's warm and as I have said before has the best views ever. Already making an appearance are Brussel's sprouts, peas, salad leaves, kalettes, tomatoes and in the veggie plot shallots and garlic have peeped through the soil to say hello. I don't want to become a gardening bore although I fear I may have passed that particular label a few weeks back, but for us, the garden is our little piece of heaven.

We are so lucky with Trevor and Jill. We only have to mention what we need to do and they work out where they can help or if they have anything to give us that lends to our projects and they are there. My poles for the runner beans etc. have been coppiced from their massive three-acre garden. Any excess plants are given over willingly, and I will be doing the same, as I deliberately sowed more than needed. The dogs have a goose egg twice a week each in their food. The goose eggs are the hardest shells I have ever come across. I literally have to hit them on the granite work surface to crack them and then sometimes twice. We have both remarked that it's like living in a tiny commune. We all help each other out. I may not be able to offer any real physical effort regarding removing the ivy off their walls due to my silly hands but another Victoria sponge for Trevor was made today and I know that will bring a smile to his little face.

We have decided to replace the Perspex, fly-splattered roof of the conservatory with a slate roof. Well, not actually slate but slate effect that looks for all intents and purposes like the genuine article. So we booked some visits from some companies that deal in this. In other words double glazing salesmen. We had three bookings. One Tuesday, one Wednesday and one today. I always expect some tall, smartly dressed young chap with slick hair to turn up with his port mantle and samples of windows and roofs. I really did not expect what did turn up.

Let's call him Gareth for this story. At around the time we were expecting the first caller there was a knock on the door and there in front of me stood Gareth. He was I would guess about fifty-five. His long blond ringlets hung in a greasy mess from halfway back from his head. He was dressed in ill-fitting grey trousers which sat precariously underneath his more than ample stomach and this was finished off by a purplish shirt that had surrendered under the strain of it all and three buttons had abandoned ship. The back of the shirt had long given up trying to stay inside his low-slung trousers and so trailed behind him covering what we were to discover when he bent down, his builder's bum. After showing him into the living room and giving him a coffee he spent an hour telling us about the Welsh bible translations and that in his opinion Thomas Thomas was a mediocre poet at best. I dare not look at Helen but when I did she had glazed over and was visiting her own planet which I must admit for the first time in twenty years I wish I could join. I subtly at first encouraged him to stay on the subject in hand but Gareth wasn't having any of it and for a while I wondered if he was a relative of Edna's such was his stubbornness. So eventually he did get onto our conservatory roof, not literally you understand, and then made the phone call to his manager who would give us a price. He must have thought Helen and I were very gullible as he started to talk to his manager about how cheap the price was and was he sure that was the price and asked if the vouchers that offered us a magnificent discount would still be viable for us, blah, blah, blah. Yes, they would, the manager intoned but only if we ordered today. I could go on but you get the picture. Typically con-man sales speak. So for our smallish conservatory, a Victorian three-section effort, they wanted... Are you sitting down? Ten thousand pounds.

Helen and I managed to keep our jaws from hitting the floor and collapsing into hysterical laughter. So to sum up, after three hours of enduring this scripted charade he left with nothing and we did our best to get rid of the body odour smell left in his wake. We cancelled the rest of the visits as we felt traumatised and at our age can't afford to waste any more time. So Archangel Trevor got his builder friend to come round tonight and within ten minutes he had measured, told us he would get back to us and we feel he is going to be a lot more realistic in his pricing.

In summation do not even think about replacing your conservatory roof unless you are in good health and of sound mind and if you are, get a builder.

We have had so many laughs over the last few days mostly involving our neighbours.

We decided to dress up Trevor's suit of armour that proudly sits in front of his wall on the lane leading up to his house. When he bought it we did scratch our heads in bewilderment somewhat as it is not everyone who sticks one of these outside their house, however, as it was Trevor we only had a slight scratch and put the rest down to the fact he is barking mad. As he had jokingly said one of the reasons he had bought it was to 'keep the gays out' we were determined to play some sort of prank on him and 'Raymondo' as he had been named.. The best we could come up with was to transform 'Ray' into a more feminine version and await what happened.

Helen and I sorted out some old clothes but had to cut them up the back and secure them around the figure with clothes pegs. We were cackling and giggling during the transformation of Raymondo and sounded like a cross between old hags and silly schoolgirls. The funniest part was when the skirt went on and Raymondo's great big iron boots stuck out from underneath. Pleased with our achievement we waited with bated breath for Trevor to return from his excursion.

Trevor had been out all day and was due home around five o'clock. As we can see all approaching vehicles from our kitchen window we finally saw him approach and went outside and stood on the doorstep to see what happened. His car passed our drive and proceeded on up the lane until he came into sight of his newly converted statue and his car came to a sudden halt. By this time we were in fits of laughter and all we could see was the back of his head in the driving seat staring at the masterpiece we had created. Finally his head slowly turned in our direction and we could see he was smiling broadly; he got out of his car and proclaimed we had turned Ray into a transvestite and he loved it and asked if we could leave it like that! You had to be there, I guess, but we thoroughly enjoyed being daft and trust him to want to keep it like that.

So Easter Sunday, we decided to attend the local church and when I looked at their website it stated that today everyone was meeting at the old post office in Talley village and following a donkey. Trevor had decided to bring along Thomas and we all duly left in time. When we got there nothing was occurring. No people and no donkey.

'I think we have missed it,' I said, looking around.

'Nope, the donkey's not been here,' Trevor said confidently, looking at the floor. 'There's no pee and poo.'

So off we trundled to the actual church and I decided to venture in. The church itself is small but exquisite. The whole rear of the church has the most amazing stained-glass windows and each pew is enclosed with its own little door. I approached a man who looked like he belonged to the clergy.

'Good morning,' I ventured. 'Happy Easter. Have we missed the donkey?'

He looked at me for a couple of seconds, almost pitying me.

'Yes, by a week. Palm Sunday was last Sunday, you know, Jesus entering the city on a donkey.'

The penny dropped with me and I turned a wonderful shade of magenta.

'Ah yes,' I said, shuffling my feet and staring at the floor. 'How embarrassing.' He laughed and told me he forgot most things too and not to worry as the service was in half an hour for Easter Sunday. I thanked him and sidled out of the church trying to maintain as much dignity as I could muster.

I told Helen and Trevor and I have to say Trevor looked relieved that he didn't have to sit through the service and he drove us home. Once home we got into our car and went back to the church. The service was lovely and everyone so friendly. We will go back.

After church we went to Trevor and Jill's for brunch and it was a lovely time. We all sat around eating and chatting as usual and somehow evidently I am cooking a Thai meal for us all next Sunday. However, every time Trevor looks at me now he rolls his eyes, tuts and says, 'Effing donkey.'

Work continues in the garden; I have a feeling that will be a never-ending job. Our arch is now installed and roses ordered. Plans for our seating area are coming along nicely and all in all we are doing well. We could have really done with some nice donkey manure for those roses but never mind, there is always next Palm Sunday.

CHAPTER 21

In between the torrential rain, April showers and biting wind we have ventured into the garden. I have a dozen and one things to get on with regarding the vegetable sowing and growing process. Helen always tells me a list of things that she has planned but in reality she wanders off topic regularly and finds all sorts of jobs to do that always involve dragging me away from my focus.

Yesterday for instance, whilst I was happily sowing in the greenhouse and planning the compost heap layout she decided that a large branch that overhangs the proposed seating area had to go. So as she is scared of heights and struggles using a saw I ended up about sixteen feet off the ground up an ancient wooden ladder brandishing said saw. Once in position I held onto the trunk with one arm and with the other hand started sawing. This branch was about five to six inches in diameter and about fifteen feet long. I looked down when I was about halfway through to see Helen directly underneath the branch with arms outstretched in front of her.

'What are you doing?' I enquired.

'Waiting to catch the branch,' she said in all seriousness.

After having explained to her that it might not be the best idea she had ever come up with she thankfully moved and eventually when the branch came crashing down with force we were both glad she took my advice. Trevor had driven past while I was performing this task and he appeared, coming towards us, chainsaw in hand. He cut the branch up into log-sized pieces for us so we can now dry it out and use it next winter for the log burner.

I returned back to my greenhouse and finished sowing nasturtium seeds and then started on the compost heap. Armed with a drill, hammer, some screws, some wooden posts found in the dovecote and three old pallets we are now the proud owners of a three-tiered system compost area.

Gertie's broodiness has waned, thank goodness, although she is not laying at all. Yesterday morning Phoebe, who spends all of her indoor time staring out of the conservatory window scanning for anything that moves, suddenly went into a frenzy of barking and it reached a hysterical, eardrum-numbing pitch. I looked out in the direction of her manic gaze and there was a vixen drinking from our stream. The vixen was completely unperturbed by Phoebe's frenzied onslaught and made her way around the garden over to the chicken run. The strange thing is she passed at least five pheasants that use our garden as a sanctuary from the 'shoot' that takes place every week in season and made a beeline for the chooks! Edna was the first to spot her and literally jumped into the dovecote followed by the other two that are a bit slower on the uptake. The fox couldn't get at them in the run anyway so she was quite optimistic to even consider it. She then proceeded to amble around the garden sniffing and marking and generally strutting her stuff without a care in the world. By now Phoebe was apoplectic; her eyes were bulging and she had a look on her face that said, 'Section me.' Finally the vixen left and we got Phoebe to settle down with the aid of a Bonio and a lot of soothing noises. Our ears were ringing for about an hour after.

The pheasants I speak of are abundant in our garden. Every morning you can guarantee there will be at least a dozen, male and female, wandering around the lawn looking for any bird food that may have been knocked off the bird tables or dropped in flight by the smaller birds that feed daily. They are lovely birds, not indigenous of course and brought here from Asia long ago to be bred for upper-class morons to shoot for fun or nowadays a corporate bonding day. How it is imagined that getting a group of office workers out of the office for the day to kill beautiful, harmless birds, will bring about a better work-based relationship, is beyond me. When we know there is going to be a shoot we put extra feed on the ground and so do Trevor and Jill, in the vain hope we can save a few. The funny thing is Phoebe is almost used to them now. Flo pays them no or very little attention at all and although Pheebs has an instinctive drive towards chasing them she is growing to understand they are here and part of this new life she has been introduced to.

The next day was glorious here in Carmarthenshire. The sun shone all day without a hint of a cloud. Helen and I made an early start in the garden. Helen has made such a difference to the flower gardens at the front of the cottage. We now have a wooden arch installed by me and E and of course the lovely Trevor. It is opposite our front door and we will be growing a white rambling rose over it called 'Adelaide D'Orlean' – it is abundant with white flowers and is fast-growing so we hope we may have a show of roses by the end of summer.

I always start off by feeding the wild birds. It is ritualistic with me. They love the peanut butter I always put out for them on Steve's bird feeders and as I am smearing it on the pine cones the blue and great tits in particular get nearer and nearer to me, twittering like crazy between themselves as if to let each other know that food is being prepared and nearly ready. The very moment I walk away the first few swoop down and land on the feeders. By the time I have reached the bridge the feeder is covered in birds of all shapes and sizes chirping and eating in a frenzy of activity. I always smile and it makes me feel very satisfied, like a mother when she knows her baby is full and contented. We have several tables and feeders so this ritual takes a while but I actually worry if I miss it or am late!

I sowed some more seeds, astrantias and cowslips. I also inspected everything I have sown so far and it is looking good. French beans, Brussel's sprouts, salads leaves, tomatoes, cabbages etc., are all making their appearance and enjoying the warmth of the greenhouse. They will stay in there until I think the worst of the weather is behind us and then they will have to face the elements like the rest of us. I also tidied up the composting area as Helen remarked that it was looking a little like Steptoe's back yard, so armed with my new cordless drill I managed to make it look a little more acceptable. Well, as acceptable as a composting area can look.

The dogs ran around all day long and the chickens were let out of their pen to wander round the back of the garden. They strut around the garden scratching away at everything and making a complete mess. Today they spent hours by the side of the stream on the bank continually pecking and scratching. They are sweet though, when it is time to go back. I usually tempt them with some pasta and lead a trail into the pen which they follow. Once in they have their food and then as the sun is beginning to set and the foxes are starting their night-time quest for sustenance I only have to open the pen door and they know it is time for bed. They walk into their coop for the night one behind the other, clucking and grumbling, and even when I have shut the door I can still hear Edna complaining.

Some exciting news happened today regarding Helen's flower photography. Some time back, Helen's photograph of a bumble bee and an iris made its way into the Gardener's World Calendar. We went to the NEC Birmingham to see it proudly displayed on a large canvas which the BBC very kindly gave us afterwards and which now hangs in our hallway. Anyway, I digress; nearby is Farmyard Nurseries which is run by a lovely chap called Richard who has won a gold in the Chelsea Flower Show for his hellebores which are absolutely magnificent. Helen came up with an idea to showcase some of her photos and approached him regarding taking shots of his various blooms throughout the rest of the season and then compiling a calendar to be sold in his shop to promote his business and her photography. He readily agreed without wanting any profit from it, saying it would be 'fun'. Such a nice man. So another project starts. I so hope it goes well for her. Will let you know.

We went over to Trevor and Jill's this afternoon for a cup of tea and Helen gave them a hand with the removal of the ivy. I have helped but because it calls for repetitive movements of the hands and fingers, the last time I helped the joints of my hands became very red and swollen so I have been banned from helping and relegated to sweeping, clearing and tea making. However, today I was tasked with feeding the lambs. What an awful job it isn't! Armed with two bottles I made my way to their pen where they stay under the warmth of a lamp. They have an abundance of straw and everything is so clean around them. I lifted them out and they have grown so much. No more do they want to sit on my lap and drink their bottle, they stand in front of me now and I hold a bottle in each hand and they pull away at the teats and their little tails wiggle in complete satisfaction.

Evidently that is how you can tell they are receiving milk when they feed from their mothers. The tail wags furiously. If it doesn't then the farmer knows they are not feeding properly or the mother is not producing milk. The bottles were emptied in record time and I stayed for a cuddle but they were desperate to get away from this daft old woman who kept wanting to hold them. The little black and white one is more amenable for a hug, the all black one is far too independent. It is a complete joy to see these two little ones and also to know how well cared for they are. I took a photo just after I fed them and they were still looking up at me expectantly to see if there was any more in the offing but alas, no.

So both of us tonight are walking like Quasimodo and poor Helen has come a cropper a couple of times. Yesterday she banged her left elbow badly, resulting in swelling and bruising and today her shin had an argument with a shovel. She actually threw it across the patio and swore at it but I do have a feeling its intentions were not malicious. So sore and tired, we retire once more knowing, weather permitting, we shall put ourselves through it all again tomorrow. I had a stern word with the shovel so hopefully it will be in a better mood.

CHAPTER 22

I'm not entirely sure and I don't want to tempt fate but, I certainly feel the weather is improving. Take Thursday for instance, we always dress for the garden which means putting on tatty clothes with varying degrees of mud on them. So I donned my usual garb and on went the thermal vest which has been an essential item of clothing every day, however, after walking around the garden and doing various chores I realised I was overheating! So the big news Thursday was that I took off my vest! Not in the garden, you understand, I wouldn't want to expose the wildlife to such a sight but for the first time since we moved I went vestless. Vestless in Llanfwr. My dear old mum wouldn't be happy, she always told me to wear a vest, even in the heat of summer, but I threw caution to the wind and haven't put it on since. So I am officially declaring summertime.

We had a little bit of drama yesterday starring Gladys the chicken and Flo and Phoebe. The hens are out all the time now, roaming around the vegetable area of the garden. Just to explain, we have about an acre of land; the land to the front of the house is probably about three quarters of that which is the pretty part of the garden and Helen is designing and working on that. The back of the house is the rest of the land and the utility area if you like. It houses the sheds, the dovecote or hencote as it is now, the greenhouse and the vegetable plots. Dividing these two areas are our newly erected fences with two gates, one each side. Stupidly, we left one of these gates open when we let the dogs out and the hens were wandering around their part of the garden. Flo and Phoebe made a beeline for the hens and poor Gladys was chased into the corner of the garden and attempted to try and get through the sheep wire we have had installed. The hole was only big enough for her to get half her body through and so the dogs attacked her rear end. By the time Helen had reached them both dogs had a mouthful of feathers. We managed to get the dogs off and I extracted poor old Gladys from the fence. She was shaken up but OK. I could feel her poor little heart thumping as I held her close to me but when I finally put her down, Helen had thrown some food on the ground for her and she just started eating normally so we both felt she would be OK. She was, I am glad to report, strutting around albeit looking a bit dishevelled with some bald patches on her bum, but apart from that she survived!

The moral of this tale is to ensure we shut the gates! Although we felt anger towards the dogs for attacking Gladys, they are only following their instinct and we have to keep telling ourselves that they do not do anything with malice unlike us humans. We told Trevor about this incident and he is supplying us with springs to put on the gate so it shuts automatically.

Trevor seems to appear as if by magic when you need him most. I built a three-sided cupboard to cover up the Calor gas bottles which sit on the back of the house outside the kitchen window. It's worked out OK and does the job but the top of the cupboard is made of plywood covered in roofing felt. For some reason our local builders wouldn't sell us plywood to fit but sent a massive piece which I had to cut. We are talking about approximately eight feet by ten feet. I only needed a piece four feet long by three feet wide and after having drawn the template onto the plywood attempted to saw it to size. Suddenly out of nowhere Trevor appeared. Needless to say, he asked if he could help which I willingly agreed to and the job was done in a blink of an eye. This man's kindness and willingness to help sometimes reduces me to tears. He shrugs off our gratitude with a wave of the hand but I am sure he enjoys the hugs we give him.

Our new wave of visitors will be descending on us soon and so we hope the fine weather continues we are both looking forward to it. It's been a long winter and although we still have some frost to come overnight we both feel the worst has gone and the brighter, longer days are now here.

So today we spent in the sunshine in the garden. Helen has planted a hawthorn hedge all around her garden with the hope it will keep the dogs away from the fence and Phoebe barking incessantly at Trevor's dogs, and latterly the little lambs that are now running around their garden and venturing out into the lane. They are extremely cute and my heart sinks every time I see them and think they will end up on some dinner plate somewhere.

I have finished the cupboard now to go around the Calor gas bottles; I also built some wooden staging for the greenhouse and I must say I am really pleased with it. Both Helen and I will be so pleased when all the hard graft work is done, like digging holes for roses and hedging etc. She suffers nightly with sore arms and back from her labours and I shuffle around like Quasimodo on Valium. But we will get there and as I keep chanting, we don't have to do it all in the first year.

This gardening lark is certainly hard on our backs. Both of us already have dodgy backs; my back was a victim of the nursing years before the 'no lifting' policies came in and Helen's the result of a game of badminton many years ago with me which resulted in her being taken off to hospital. Since then she has always had problems. I had two prolapsed discs that take it in turns to give me a bout of sciatica now and again but all in all I think my back problems are less significant that hers. I digress, basically our backs are killing us! We have now entered for the local championships in the Best Silly Walk competition and think we do stand an excellent chance.

Regardless of the pain and agony we are going through we are enjoying our days even though we are strangely pleased when the weather forecast predicts rain for the next day as it means we can have a day off! Daft really when you think about it as we could actually just take some time out anytime we want, but we are eager to put our projects into action. Today Helen actually planted the last of the hawthorn hedging or Mayflower bushes as they are called as they flower in May. It heralds the arrival of spring, by bursting into leaf within a few days of the initial buds appearing and has an abundant and spectacular display of white, scented blossom. In the autumn it develops glossy red haws which sustain our native birds especially starlings, thrushes, blackbirds and redwings. It also supports more than 150 species of insect which are a rich food source for birds such as wrens and blue tits, so we are hoping they will all take and we will reap the rewards by enjoying the abundance of wildlife. Win-win.

We are booking our first lesson in beekeeping which starts in a few weeks, so we are looking forward to that, we just hope we can manage it as Helen has her lovely bee hive which was a leaving present when she left work, so we are keen to learn as much as we can and start our own colony. Evidently Trevor is allergic to bees so we will put the hive outside his gate… OK, we won't really, but evidently he is going along with us so I just hope he has an EpiPen!

There is a predicted heatwave hitting Wales the latter part of this week so I should imagine by Sunday both Helen and I will be in traction. We are actually looking forward to the warmer evenings as we have a semi-circular stone seating area near our stream and we have a fire pit in the centre. We aim to sit out there for a couple of hours in the evening and listen to the night-time sounds. We know we will be treated to tawny owls and barn owls. The tawny owls make that lovely twit-twoo sound but the barn owls sound like I imagine a banshee would. It's a dreadful bloodcurdling screech that pierces the night and casts an eerie feel to the blackness that surrounds you. Having no light pollution here the stars on a clear night are truly magnificent. We recognise The Plough and Orion but I really think we should learn a little more about what we are looking at as it would make the night-time spectacular even more interesting. Tonight I note the moon is a whisper-thin lunar crescent and the surrounding constellations hang next to it animated literally in the vast space that surrounds it. That vastness takes my breath away, and the tranquillity and mystery of it all never fails to make me feel infinitesimal. I can understand people's fascination with space and what lies beyond, although I have to admit that our planet alone is enough for me and there are still many things I for one need and want to learn about it.

CHAPTER 23

TS Eliot wrote in The Waste Land:

April is the cruellest month, breeding

Lilacs out of the dead land, mixing

Memory and desire, stirring

Dull roots with spring rain.

I beg on this occasion to differ with Mr Eliot as it has been so hot here that I feel we may be getting lulled into a false sense of security regarding the season. I actually did put my flip-flops on today for about four hours but soon got my boots back on as the sun went down. I do love to live dangerously.

It must be spring at least as we mowed the lawn today. Helen sat astride Delilah, the sit and ride lawnmower, and took her for her maiden voyage around the grounds, however, I got the short straw with the hand petrol mower on the vegetable side of the garden. Must rethink this for next time but I have to say it looks exceptionally nice. I did think Helen looked like Noddy though, all she needed was a pointy hat with a bell.

We have had a very busy few days and productive to say the least. The second vegetable plot is all but filled now, just the top mulch to go and it is ready for planting. We cleared the back of the garage area and made it into a seating area. Prior to that it was just concrete and old wood and rubbish, now looking resplendent with a border, reclaimed Victorian edging found stuffed behind the shed, and a newly planted climbing rose which Helen has provided wire for in order for it to ramble up the back of the garage. I made another small raised bed for the irises and ornamental bark has gone down on the ground with the tables and chairs now in place. We are happy with it and actually sat at the table today with a cup of tea for at least ten minutes. A record!

We have had bovine visitors on the field to the bottom of our garden and the side. Flo and Phoebe are in awe of them. They do not bark at them, thank goodness, but stare in wonderment at these large, silent, grass-eating beings that have wandered over to us. The cows were drinking just by our fence today from the stream. They looked at me for ages and the more I stood looking at them the more of them came over to see what the fuss was all about. In the end I guess at roughly twenty of them were all crowding around the fence to stand and gaze at this woman covered in mud and dripping with sweat (or should I say glistening?). I decided perhaps I should move before they all decided to get nearer and push our fence over and trample on my shallots. I left and they all wandered off in different directions but for that brief time we all 'had a moment'.

The hens are enjoying their freedom and have discovered the stone semicircle seating area. Inside this area is mainly just dirt and dust and today I watched them sitting in it, clawing at the ground underneath them to get to the coolness of the earth underneath. The spent a lot of the day doing this, so much so in the end I put their food in there. They are happy hens and their eggs tell the tale. The eggs we have now are medium-to-large eggs and three a day. Our cholesterol will go through the roof but the dogs are enjoying their eggy dinners a couple of times a week.

Trevor and Jill's geese are mating. The noise is deafening! Fascinating to watch as the ganders clean themselves up before breeding, they preen themselves or take a good dust bath. The also do a lot of wing spreading, stretching and flapping, along with gentle and aggressive pecking of their prospective female. During all this time they are making a honking noise at the same decibel level of a jet plane. The female goose makes a really low-pitched honk whereas the gander is high-pitched. Trevor has three ganders and three females and they mate for life. I can't wait to see the goslings when they hatch.

*

Well, the hot spell didn't last long, although I suppose for April we are asking too much, however, come May I shall be insisting on more warm sunny days. I've already written to my MP. So, the flip-flops have been told to stand down until further notice but are positioned at the front of the wardrobe to be ready to redeploy at a moment's notice.

I must admit to being impressed with the weather forecasting these days. Long gone it seems is the Michael Fish 'Great Storm of 1987' faux pas and technology has now given us hour by hour accurate weather predictions. Take today for instance, I read it would rain until about 11am and it did, then just dull and cloudy until 4pm, it was, and then two hours' sunshine and back to being dull again. Spot on, Met Office! I am hoping they will give me the winning lottery numbers in the near future but then I guess everyone would have them! It is also telling me not to expect any more frosts this year so I can plant out my vegetable plants from the greenhouse but Trevor keeps telling me not to be lulled into a false sense of frost-free security, so they will stay put for now.

Thanks to the bovine visitors our stream has a nice layer of cow poop floating in places. They need less fat in their diet, perhaps? It is quickly dispersing but it doesn't do anything for the ambience or the picturesque view we did have. It looks like a slurry tank. There is not much life going on in there to be honest but who could blame it? We have had frogs, water boatmen, the usual water snails, larvae etc. but no fish or anything really interesting. It is crystal-clear though, (apart from the poo patches) and there are lots of aquatic plants growing in it which makes it look quite pretty… I repeat, except for the poo.

We watched the London Marathon this morning as the wet weather prevented us from gardening. A record number evidently turned out for it this year. I cannot believe that some people ran dressed as Paddington Bear or Big Ben in that heat and actually finished! Hats off to them. My youngest son and his wife ran the Brighton Marathon last week and managed to raise in excess of £500 for their chosen charity which helps disabled children in Kent where they live. I am very proud of them both. I would have loved to have achieved something like that and I note an eighty-seven-year-old ran today! Hope for me yet, although the rheumatoid arthritis might not like it. A huge well done to all those people who run marathons and the like and the thousands and thousands of pounds, if not millions, they have raised for their charities that fills the gap in the shortfall of funding that this Government fails to provide or has drastically cut in its wake.

We actually went over to Trevor and Jill's last night for a BBQ. Trevor was the head chef with his ready-prepared chicken kebabs. I had made a salad and some mixed rice with ginger to take over and there were other veggie options on offer too. It was a lovely evening, sitting in their huge grounds, chatting, laughing and just sharing. By 9:30pm though, it was so dark we couldn't see each other and it had turned remarkably cold so we all said goodnight and headed home. Jill's daughter has a friend staying there who used to live in Heathfield, East Sussex, where Helen and I lived for a few years. Talk about small world! The poor girl also had juvenile rheumatoid arthritis which she contracted following a bout of tonsillitis aged eleven. She limped quite badly and my heart went out to her. I expect at my age to have these aches and pains, although not so many I must add, however, at eighteen and having had it for seven years already, I realised how lucky I am to have developed it in my late fifties. Thankfully she is on the very best treatment that the medical profession can offer.

*

The hens' house and pen has had a makeover. The floor is now covered in straw as they have removed every last blade of grass and it makes it for easier chicken poo shovelling. They only spend a fraction of their day in there now anyway but the straw and poo goes on the compost, so a win-win.

Flo and Phoebe continue to enjoy life; Phoebe may be having a laryngectomy soon if her excessive barking continues! This morning she went into an absolute barking fest over a resident vole we have that lives in the brickwork surrounding of all things our septic tank which just happens to be in a direct line with Phoebe's gaze from the conservatory. The vole, has a brilliant vantage point as above its abode is one of the bird tables and so seeds regularly are dropped or pushed off the table, thus giving the vole its own supply of seeds, a bit like a drive-thru McDonald's only healthier. I watched it for ages; it pops its head out, looks around to see if the coast is clear and then gathers up its bounty and disappears in a flash. However brief this occurrence is, though, it is enough for Phoebe to become hysterical and almost cry in frustration that she can't do a thing about it but observe. I swear the vole gave her 'the finger' at one point!

Helen and I were due to go to the hairdressers last Thursday for the first time since we have been here. Her appointment was at 10am and mine at 11:30am. I didn't want to hang around for an hour and a half in Llanfwr waiting for my turn so we agreed to go separately. So as usual Helen was cutting it fine getting out of the door. We always have a last-minute mayhem session when Helen goes anywhere that she has to be on time for. I must admit to never having met anyone with such a disregard for punctuality as Helen. It's not that she does it deliberately, she just doesn't 'get it'.

So rushing out of the door she tries to open her car and nothing happens. Her key battery had died. So I told her I would forego my appointment and she should take my car as her hair needs were greater than mine. I tie my hair up most of the time so really it wasn't urgent, whereas Helen's hair, being short desperately needed a restyle. So I went in to get my car keys and they were not hanging on the hook; that set off another frantic ten minutes tearing the house to bits looking for them when I suddenly came across the spare keys, so finally off she went. I found my keys eventually in her coat pocket... I'll just leave that there. I must say though, it was worth having a near nervous breakdown, a near stroke and possible start of divorce proceedings in the end because she came home and her hair looked wonderful. I am so pleased she has found a hairdresser that cuts well. She had seen the same hairdresser in Sussex for years, so this was a great find. She looks lovely. I on the other hand look like I have been dragged through the proverbial bush backwards but hopefully the next appointment I have will be mishap-free and some of these lank locks will be lying on the floor of the hairdressers in the near future.

CHAPTER 24

Well, April is certainly living up to its name here. One minute we are in the garden happily doing what we do and the next we are standing around like someone has just tipped a bucket of water over our heads. Hey-ho, this too shall pass.

Helen embarked on her first toe dip into beekeeping yesterday accompanied by Trevor. The venue was the Royal Botanical Gardens and was intended to give a small taster of what is involved in this amazing hobby.

Helen gained a lot of insight into what it would entail and also the commitment needed to embark on this venture. Personally we are only looking at helping bees rather than any financial gain from the honey they produce. Evidently the last two summers' weather has devastated the Welsh bee population and we need to boost their numbers significantly and ensure a healthy environment for them. We are going to source locally to see if any local beekeepers will give us the benefit of their experience and help us on our way to be able to have our own hives and help nature as much as possible, with the added bonus of some toast and honey!

It is nearing the time when all my greenhouse babies will leave their nursery and face the elements of the 'Welsh Summer', an oxymoron if ever I heard one! Evidently as previously mentioned the last two summers here have been less than tropical so we are hoping for some improvement on that score this year. The only thing that is certain is that we will not have a water shortage. No wonder our water rates are so low!

We have two more gigantic, enormous bags of compost being delivered this week on pallets so that should be the final topping on the veggie beds and subsequent years will need only mulching. I feel under a lot of pressure after all this planning and preparation to produce vegetables and fill the new freezer waiting patiently in the garage to spring into action and preserve the mountains of blanched veg I have grown for it. I just hope we get more than five oddly shaped carrots and a few spuds. Watch this space!

The evenings have been cold enough to light our wood burner each evening and the other night I sat on the couch, Earl Grey in hand, and watched the flames as the sun started to dip behind the cottage. The silhouette of the trees in the garden started to loom through the lattice arched windows of the living room which always give an ecclesiastical feel to the house and the owls hooted backwards and forwards as if to summon the advent of the night. Our pipistrelle bats started their night-time air display in earnest, flying in circles around and around the front of the cottage in search of moths and any flying insect lured out by the call of the darkness. It was quite magical and I feel I should pinch myself at times to ensure that it is real and we are living here amongst the very best that nature can offer. Some called us mad when we first announced we were going to move here, others called us brave, but the ones that said we were lucky were the most accurate. Maybe we are all three, mad, brave and lucky? Whatever we are it has been worth all the stress, the upheaval, the doubts and the worries and we are still only bordering on six months into this chapter of our lives.

The sun is shining as I type and a new day lies ahead waiting for us to venture out and see what mayhem and mischief we can get up to today. I think Helen will have to become Noddy again and get Delilah out of her shed as the grass has already sprung up to where it was before last week's cut. I will clean out the chickens and prevent Gladys and Gertie from brooding. They are both doing it now, only Edna is happily scratching around the garden without a maternal thought in her body. And I might, just might get those babies out of their cots. Who out there is betting there will be a frost tonight? The law of sod may rear its smug face but I am going to chance it.

I nearly alerted the media, as it hasn't rained for two days! We are not overly confident that this will last, however, the forecast is good for the next week. The downside is I have a horrible cold which hit me full pelt on Friday and since then I have had a banging headache, constant bunged up nose and a gland under my chin is swollen and sore to the touch. Apart from that I am hunky dory. Needless to say I have been taking it easy and poor Helen has had the brunt of the gardening, although my part of the garden is under control to a large degree.

Helen does so well with the gardening. We purchased a 'Doggy Dooley'. This for the uninitiated is basically a cess pit for dog poo. We had to dig a hole about three feet deep to place it in which Helen did most of… Boy, that woman can dig! I put the thing together and the way it works is supposed to be completely environmentally friendly. As we have two dogs we need to add two enzyme tablets a week and six gallons of water twice a week. The poo just dissolves and there is no odour. So far so good. Although we still have to go around the garden and collect the 'dooleys', all we then have to do is drop the doo-doo in! I recommend it to anyone who has a dog and don't worry any future guests, it is nowhere near the produce-growing part of the garden!

Delilah has been for another spin and she does her job well. Helen is in her element and we are now getting into a really good routine with all the jobs that need doing. The really hard stuff is more or less done now. I still have a metal arch to put up near the stream but that will be easy compared to the wooden one we had to erect. We have become experts at applying Postcrete and cementing things in. I walk around with my new drill in my hand fixing things, Helen moves plants around, digs holes and between us we make a really good combination.

We visited the nursery where Helen is going to take photos to make the calendar she is hoping to sell and left her other calendars for the owner to see her work. Fingers crossed he is happy and she can start. We are also hoping to enter into a competition later in the year just to see how we do. It is to do with plants and gardens so who knows?

We have heard a cuckoo over the past week and when you think it has made its way over from Africa it amazes me. Cuckoos from the

UK probably travel down through central Europe to the south of Italy, where they feed up before crossing to Africa. Some scientists think that they then cross the Mediterranean and Sahara in a single flight of more than 1,875 miles! Can you imagine? Once here they find a nest of a dunnock or meadow pipit, usually, and lay their egg then sod off! The poor host bird then loses all her eggs once the cuckoo hatches which it cleverly does before the other eggs, and then it pushes them all out of the nest, then this poor little host bird feeds this walloping great chick until it fledges. This young bird then leaves around August and flies all the way back to Africa. How? I can't get to my car door without a sat nav; how do these birds find Africa? And we think we are clever! *Pfft!*

We have visitors for the next two weekends which we are both looking forward to and hopefully the weather will be nice enough for us to be able to enjoy the surroundings without getting wet! After that, quite a few visitors are making their way here. We are very lucky that so many lovely people want to come to see us.

Finally I have submitted the planning permissions for the work we need to carry out on the conservatory and the dovecote. I have never come across such bureaucratic nonsense in all my days. I needed plans for the area and plans for the site, which actually amounts to the same thing! Drawings of proposed work, what materials will be used, etc. etc. What's the betting it comes back as not complete and they need to know the blood group of the builders or something?

So May is here and the announcement of the month is... drum roll please... the runner beans are out!

And that is about as exciting as it gets. To be honest the decision was made for me as they had become so tall and were starting to suffer from the heat of the greenhouse so out they went, followed closely by the carrots.

We had a delivery of eighteen hundred litres of 'Veggie Gold' compost to finally finish off the vegetable plot. Yesterday saw us filling up the trugs for the root veg and we did a good job of it if I may say so myself, and so all the little carrot plants have found a new home in one of them. So hopefully the frost will not return and the garden can finally leave its proverbial vest off now May is here!

The weather has been changeable to say the least but very indicative of the time of year, however, we are promised a heatwave this Bank Holiday which I am not holding my breath about. We have friends coming on Friday so the house is going through its usual pre-visitor clean and tidy up. Helen and I are very different when it comes to tidiness. I am the one who likes everything tidy on the outside or as my dad used to call me, 'Fur coat and no drawers,' but the drawers in question are a tad messy. I throw everything in cupboards and hope for the best. My underwear drawer for instance looks like the leftovers from a jumble sale after the crowds have sifted and plundered through it. Helen, however, leaves everything lying around. To demonstrate, if I raise my gaze to look at her chest of drawers in our bedroom to see what is stacked upon it, the result is various photos in frames not arranged in any order or facing the right way for that matter, a large toilet bag hanging open like a gaping gob about to spew all its contents on the floor, a see-through plastic bag with goodness knows what in it, and a pair of slippers (don't ask) and these are perched precariously on top of a pile of books and a pamphlet for Christmas gift ideas. The contents of this dresser, however, are arranged so each and every item of clothing is in order of colour and neatly folded, even her knickers. I am in awe of her drawer OCD and sometimes try to emulate it, spending a half day with all my stuff piled on the bed and then neatly replaced. Within about three days, give or take an hour or two, the whole thing is back to square one. Summing up, somehow we jog along with our differences. Me, following her around and picking things up and putting them away in no particular order and her never going near the inside of any of my cupboards for fear of a mental breakdown. It works.

Today we are off to Llanfwr (just noticed the predictive text on this tried to change Llanfwr into Landfill... a bit harsh, I thought) to shop for this weekend and then this afternoon no doubt back in the garden heaving around more compost. I have to say I will be glad when this is finally done as I am getting a bit cheesed off with humping around wheelbarrows full of the stuff but a necessary evil, I am afraid.

We are now the proud owners of three brooding hens. All three, Gertie, Gladys and Edna are now sitting in their luxury home, flicking through *OK* magazines and watching daytime TV and refusing to move or work for their living, hence no eggs. So this morning they were all thrown out of their penthouse and I have shut the door so they can't get back in. They have the whole of the garden to forage around in so hopefully this broodiness will pass and they can go back to laying. *Women!*

Looking out onto the garden now that spring has coaxed all the leaves out of the trees and shrubs and the plants have decided it is safe enough to emerge from the cold earth that is slowly warming, the landscape around us is becoming lush and full of varying shades of green. Everything has taken on a new shape, a new colour and what was brown and stark has now become softer and more welcoming than before. This is one of the reasons we came, amongst many, to enjoy the very best nature can offer us, and talking of nature, we have a hedgehog! We haven't named it yet as its gender is uncertain and I for one am not picking it up to have a look, however, the nameless one is a welcome visitor and we suspect there are more out there. We have about three hedgehog houses placed around the garden in quiet positions so hopefully they have moved in and are enjoying the good life... as are we.

The weekend with our friends Anna and Gerry was a very relaxing, chilled-out time had by all. We spent most of the day Saturday in the garden with everyone pitching in. Anna proved to be a chicken whisperer and managed to get them all out of bed and foraging for food. Gerry has found a new occupation as our groundsman and our lawn looks like one of the royal parks. He meticulously steered the lawnmower to produce straight lines and by the happy look on his little face he thoroughly enjoyed himself. Well done, Gerry!

In the evening we all went out for a scrumptious meal and came home and stargazed. The sky was crystal-clear and made even more special by the appearance of a shooting star. I used an app on my phone that tells you where the planets and satellites are and the names of every star above your head, it is fascinating. Jupiter was so clear in the sky but without the app I would have just mistaken it for another star. It makes you feel infinitesimal compared to the endless universe and beyond. I have never really been into stargazing but living here with no light pollution, as the sky gets darker the night sky starts to dazzle us with its show of thousands of celestial bodies that are there constantly but can only be seen when light sources disappear.

Anna and Gerry left us in the afternoon to return home and despite the heat Helen and I decided to garden, Helen busy in her part of her garden and me rescuing some scorched, shrivelled-up brown things from the greenhouse. To date the lettuces, cabbages, broad beans, peas, carrots, shallots, red and brown onions are all out in their permanent beds. It's very satisfying to watch them grow and see them turn the brown beds into green carpets. There are still a lot of veggies to plant out so I envisage some hard work to follow in the coming weeks. Finally though, I have topped off the second large veggie bed with compost and it is ready to receive its occupants. So relieved it is finally accomplished.

The sun shone for the next few days and we actually had to take it easy until mid-afternoon because of the heat. We just pottered about for a while and ate lunch al fresco and then as the day seemed to be cooling we got stuck in and did some grafting but thankfully we have passed the worst.

The chickens have stopped laying altogether. We chuck them out of their pen so they stop brooding but they pathetically huddle in the doorway of the dovecote, all three of them looking like old ladies at a bus stop sheltering from a storm. It actually makes me feel sorry for them and I am always tempted to just let them back in but I would not be doing them any favours if I did as they starve themselves, as said before. Trevor is now supplying us with eggs which he is happy to do as he has more than Tesco, Sainsbury's and the Co-Op. We gave the last of ours to Anna and Gerry, willingly I must add as they were piling up, and there are only so many eggs you can or should for that matter eat.

This week will see the installation of our wooden blinds in the kitchen and once again we shall tackle the planning applications that have been spat back at us yet again as being written by a moron. We have now found out how to draw to scale, written a Heritage statement, graded building planning applications and pulled out most of our hair; the remainder has gone grey and we have upped the tranquillisers (joke). We have also developed a twitch similar to the Inspector Dreyfus character brilliantly played by Herbert Lom in the Pink Panther films. So once again we shall endeavour to try and get it right and send them back. At least we are giving the pedants in the council planning department a good laugh. I can almost hear their exasperation in the emails they send back, once they can steady their hands enough because of the guffawing. Wish us luck.

CHAPTER 25

We have a gate with a flip-up hook and eye latch attached to a very old post. In a hurry I flipped up the latch and my thumb collided with the post and the upward motion drove a splinter into my thumb. You know straight away when you are in a bit of trouble and despite Helen's efforts to get the bugger out with a needle and scalpel it just resulted in a lot of blood and a bit of swearing... Well OK, a little more than a bit.

So by the night-time I found the thumb had swollen and turned a lovely shade of shiny red and by the morning it was clear I was in trouble. I phoned our wonderful GP surgery to see if they could deal with it or should I schlepp over to Carmarthen hospital. The receptionist booked me in straight away and after seeing the GP and getting some antibiotics the practice nurse did the deed. I could almost see her excitement as she dug away with the needle and scalpel and because she wasn't Helen I didn't make a fuss. The nurse retrieved the log from my thumb and almost danced around the treatment room in triumph. I thanked her and sloped off home, relieved the splinter was finally out. Needless to say I have caught said thumb on everything I possibly could; the dogs have smashed into it, I have caught it in drawers etc. The saying 'stuck out like sore thumb' sprang to my mind more than once.

The weather has been lovely still. We did have some showers but nothing significant. The stream in the garden has partially dried up and much to Phoebe's delight she can now walk nearly the length of it up to her elbows in thick, black gunk. Sweet. The chickens have also been eyeing it as a possibility to cross...

Q. Why did the chicken cross the stream?

A. To get to my bloody vegetable plot and eat all the nice young plants growing.

So another conundrum rears its head and I am going to have to watch them carefully. They are still not laying any eggs, still huddling in the dovecote doorway when they have been ousted from their nest. Helen and I are at a loss as to what to do to get them back on track so to speak. Edna does show some signs of snapping out of her hormone-induced stupor but Gertie and Gladys remain resolute in their quest to hatch something even if it is each other's heads.

We had a lovely weekend with Helen's Uncle Owen and his wife Sally. They travelled across from their home in Westminster in London on Saturday and left today, Sunday, after lunch. A short but sweet visit and enjoyed by us all. It is especially nice for Helen to be able to have a family connection again, something she obviously has missed since losing her family and finding her uncle has given her a connection she thought was lost when her father died. She knew her paternal grandfather had another family by his second wife but had never known her half uncle or aunt growing up, so through my search on Ancestry her Aunty Sally got in touch and Bob's your uncle, or in this case Owen. We had a really good time talking about London, our childhoods and the old traditions and ways being long gone now but still fresh to us people of a certain age, some bittersweet, some just fun and others emotive but comforting at the same time. So a huge thank you to them both for making such an effort to see us.

Out next visitor is my daughter who is coming for a week and I am very much looking forward to that. She is like us in many ways when it comes to our wildlife interests and I am keen to take her to see the butterfly house at the Royal Botanical Gardens of Wales. I am sure we will also go and see the red kites feeding again, I could never tire of that spectacle and if I ever do, shoot me!

The week ahead weather-wise looks promising and tomorrow we

hope to go for a nice walk around the river with our cameras to see what we can capture. We haven't really had the time until now to be able to indulge in some photography but with the fine weather and the garden sort of under control we can afford some time out to indulge ourselves in one of our favourite hobbies. Fingers crossed we will get something to capture.

The field next door has been covered in sheep and the smallest lambs ever. I love just sitting in the conservatory watching them. To be honest sheep are pretty boring. They graze, walk a bit, graze some more, poo and make a few obligatory bleating noises and that's the sum total of their activity. Having said all that I really don't know what else they can do really, so maybe I am being too judgemental to sheep. The magpies and jackdaws target them as they are a sort of mobile café to them. When I say 'mobile' I mean they could be mobile if they decided to actually move. The birds sit on their backs and relieve the sheep of their ticks. It is at this juncture I am grateful I am of another species. The sheep I think are reasonably grateful to the birds for clearing the parasites off their backs because they seem oblivious to them or at least do not seem to mind. So it's a win,-win situation. The sheep lose a few ticks and the birds get an effortless lunch.

Exploring our surroundings as we can on a daily basis makes us both feel we are on holiday. Just a few minutes' walk as some of our visitors can testify, are the most amazing views. A walk by the river produces sights and sounds only nature can conjure up. The high-pitched unmistakable song of the kingfisher, busy bees flying backwards and forwards in search of pollen, signalling to other bees when they have found an abundance of flowers to feast upon. The rushing of the river that in places drowns out all other noise and brings about ambient sounds that even defeats my tinnitus at its loudest. Remnants of small waterfalls that appear on the banks of the other side of the country lane indicating their presence by trickles of water that have gouged out a path leading to their ultimate goal of joining the river. All these sights and sounds surround us as we take a pre-lunch stroll. We look back over the fields and there lies Ty Mawr, standing humbly in the background, our washing on the line, waving to us in the wind, just to remind us both, it's not a dream, we are home.

We have had some glorious weather over the past week and have made the most of it. The garden is looking cared for and we have developed skills we never knew existed. Example; a delivery driver a few weeks ago decided he could do a three point turn in our narrow lane and ended up hitting our gate post. We have a very heavy farm gate that needs to be opened and closed every time we go out. Due to this collision the gate had dropped down and despite Trevor tightening the bolts to lift it, the gate remained broken and to open it each time was a feat of strength and determination.

Helen discovered that a post very nearby was the key to lifting the gate and between us we managed to get this post back far enough, propping it in position with an iron bar found in the dovecote and then another support post sunk into the ground and cemented in. It worked. We now have a working gate again and very chuffed we both are too. Even our very Welsh building supplier remarked that he thought we both were 'coming along nicely'. Not bad for two old birds, eh?

The gardening continues. Most of the vegetables are now facing the elements in the beds, just a few still languishing in the greenhouse refusing to grow up. It is a never-ending task for both of us. Some days we wonder if we have taken on too much and on these days we tend to sit in the garden and soak up the environment and look around us; this confirms to us that yes, we have done the right thing and every ache, every pain, and every time we walk bent double because we can't straighten our backs after digging or kneeling, is thoroughly worth it.

We visited the nursery that Helen is making the calendar for today and met up with the owner, Ralph. He was delighted with the portfolio of photographs Helen had left to enable him to see her work. He seems really keen and told Helen to feel right at home in the nursery and go wherever she wants to on his grounds. Another employee took her to the nursery perimeter to see a view which stretched across a wooded area. He said each morning when he arrives at work he heads for this area to soak up the view and look at the mist that always forms over the trees. This kind of mist forms when the sky is clear and the wind speeds are low. It's actually called radiation fog, a sinister-sounding name but actually just means that when the sky is clear at night, land surfaces radiate heat to space and if there is no wind, droplets of dew form on, for example, grass. If there is a very gentle breeze, the tiny water droplets are stirred upwards to form a shallow layer of radiation fog. It's very atmospheric and just adds another layer to the beauty of this countryside.

We had a very near miss yesterday. We decided to allow Phoebe and Flo over to the vegetable side of the garden as the stream had dried up and the hens had taken themselves off for an afternoon siesta. What we failed to realise is that there is a gap in the fence that is usually covered by water, this leads onto the neighbouring field which is currently occupied by ewes and their little lambs. Phoebe wasted no time in planning her escape and I just so happened to look up from weeding as there was an almighty racket coming from the field. A flash of white far too quick for any sheep went past me and a stampede of sheep ensued. I ran as fast as I could and got over the fence into the field and gave chase, screaming, 'Phoebe!' at the top of my voice but she gave no hint that anything I was screaming at her had penetrated her focus. She didn't, I am relieved to say, attempt to hurt them but was rounding them up, directing them left and right.

The noise was deafening from the sheep; at one point she directed about fifty sheep towards me and I started to think that this was the way I was going to end my days, trampled to death by a load of sheep and lambs, however at the last minute they changed direction. Eventually after about ten minutes which seemed more like ten hours she got bored and wanted to go home. Flo during all this was clueless as to what was going on and just stood in one spot squinting through the fencing to see what all the fuss was about. Thank goodness for daft boxers! Phoebe's escapade came to an abrupt end when she ran slap bang into Helen who managed to grab her collar. Helen and I got Phoebe over the fence and Helen followed her. I decided to go back to the fence that I had climbed over only to find the ground was higher this side and in an attempt to climb over I landed the other side face first in the compost heap.

Now I don't know if any of you can image what it is like to be half buried in week old grass cuttings and all the vegetable and garden waste that had been put on there but suffice to say I was highly fragrant when I extracted myself from it. The narrow escape was that within seconds after flailing around like a beached whale in compost the farmer arrived on his quad bike to see what the kerfuffle was about. By this time Helen had got both dogs in hand and was showering Phoebe with the hosepipe as she was covered in sheep poo, and I nonchalantly wandered up the garden as though nothing had happened. We dare not tell him as farmers have the right to shoot dogs that worry sheep and as both Helen and I perceived this as a 'one off' as we have now ensured the gap is Phoebe-proof, we have decided to keep it to ourselves. I have now booked Phoebe on an EasyJet flight back to Zante… As if.

CHAPTER 26

I cannot believe this weather! After listening to all the stories about the Welsh weather and even one of my neighbours telling me about two weeks of sunshine ago that the three days of sun we had then was 'it'. Well he was wrong, I am thrilled to say.

We have definitely made the most of it. I now have white flip-flop marks on my feet; my tan stops halfway up my legs due to cropped trousers. I have a circle of tan on my neck and my face and arms are now the colour of Coco Pops and around the same texture. Helen is equally tanned but looks better than me. For some unknown reason the bags under my eyes get tanned first, so I end up, all in all, looking ridiculous. I considered wearing a ski mask when I go out but in this heat I figured it would only draw more attention to myself, so barefaced it is.

We haven't stopped working in the garden, it really is a full-time job; coupled with the house which fortunately is pretty easy to keep clean and all the other chores life throws at you, we never seem to stop although having said all that we do eat in the garden sometimes and also sit and have tea and coffee etc., so I am technically lying.

Our stream has dried up completely. It's actually a drainage ditch fed from the surrounding farmland, but I like to call it our 'babbling brook'... I am slightly deluded, I feel. It does look pretty when it has water in it but at the moment it is bone dry and the dogs and chickens run up and down it. Edna, the hen, is adorable. She has taken to following me around the garden. Wherever I go, about five paces behind is Edna. She sees me enter that side of the garden and literally runs towards me. My stupid brain likes to believe it's because she loves me but my sensible brain knows it is because she thinks I may have food. They are all back on the spaghetti and laying one egg a day but Edna and Gertie are still refusing to earn their keep. Gorgeous isn't everything, Edna, get laying!

The trees are all out now in full bloom; every tree has turned from their stark, brown, skeletal form into a lush green flourishing canopy of leaves, catkins and blossom. It has changed the view of the gardens and surrounding countryside completely. Every shrub and bush has now become varying shades of reds, greens, oranges and some deep mauve. One field in the distance is so full of bluebells it is completely blue to look at. The previous owners of Ty Mawr have obviously planted so many different varieties of flora and now we are starting to see everything spring into life and treat us to its splendour, revealing and exposing all the very best that nature has to offer. I often just amble around the garden's borders to see what new treat has arrived. Today I noticed we have an abundance of wild strawberries; these when they ripen are so tiny and sweet. We freeze them into ice cubes and they cheer up even tap water on a hot day.

Our bird life is also increasing, so far I have counted twenty-seven different species as garden visitors or spotted flying over. Last Sunday we were treated to a peregrine falcon soaring high above the house – a wonderful sight to behold.

Our first job of the day after feeding the dogs, the chickens and sometimes ourselves is to go around the grounds and fill up the feeders. I could actually do this more than once in a day as they have cleaned out most of them by mid-afternoon but they also have to find other food sources rather than become totally reliant on garden feeders, so I resist the urge to top them up, hard for me as I feed everything that moves. I so love to cook and create that it spills over onto anything that has a mouth and an appetite!

Well, the rain came but it was warm rain at least. The wind at the moment feels like someone is pointing a hairdryer in our direction treating us to a warm blast of air now and again; the word is balmy. The rain poured and treated the garden to a good soaking and in response the vegetables and plants are looking splendid so we are not complaining.

It's been a funny few days really. Due to the wet weather our usual routine of gardening all day, eating and drinking outdoors etc. has been disrupted and we found ourselves staring at walls a bit bored. Yesterday I had to take to my bed due to a horrid flare-up of my rheumatoid arthritis which is still bad today although the fatigue that accompanies it isn't so bad and I managed to do a few things. It sounds pathetic, but even to open a jar yesterday had me beat such was the pain in my hands and wrists. Typing is hurting now but bearable. I truly hate this disease but I know there is so much worse out there to be had so perspective reigns.

Today we tackled two boxes that ended up in the shed from our move. We had a good idea of what was in them, mostly double- or treble-ups on kitchenware and the like. We had in effect, four homes put into one – Helen's mum and dad's stuff, her sister's, mine and Helen's so we have found we have too much of everything. Coupled with the fact I am a gadget freak and Helen is a shopaholic, we discovered we had plethora of plastic food containers, none with lids, lids without their bottoms, bits of things that fit nothing or do nothing and neither of us know what their original purpose in life was, you get the picture. So for the last ten years we have been promising ourselves we will do a car boot sale and get rid of the stuff we really do not need but someone else might. Surely there must be hundreds of people out there that collect Tupperware lids? So perched on stools in the shed with the two dogs coming in and out bemused as to why we were taking up residence in a shed, we set about sorting through the boxes. Stuff we could use, stuff we couldn't bear to throw away or sell, stuff for the car boot and finally stuff for the tip.

We have dozens of CDs, and DVDs and I am not sure anyone will buy these as Netflix and Amazon have probably replaced the need but hopefully some people are still in the market for them.

It was also a very emotive experience, sifting through memories, Helen coming across a beautiful picnic set her sister Daphne bought for herself when she was with Helen in Croydon, its contents still in the original packaging as the retirement it was meant for was snatched away from her by an aggressive cancer. She retired in the

October and died the following September with nine months of that taken up with the illness, the diagnosis, the chemotherapy and eventually her passing. We both stood there staring at the unused, unwrapped plates, cutlery, napkins and cups with a little pair of salt and pepper pots that gave a promise of sandwiches, salads and plastic cups of tea under a tree or on the beach, relaxing on a hot day, time stretching ahead after a lifetime of working hard. We both felt the tears and the anger and hurt, Helen holding her chest to try and comfort the aching heart she carries around with her day after day.

There were two Laura Ashley plates belonging to Helen's mum who passed so long ago now, these have now been washed and placed in our home, too precious to be anywhere else.

Helen's father kept a yearly diary dating back to 1942. We have them all. They give a fascinating insight to his life back then, his time in the Grenadier Guards during WW2, everyday thoughts of a young unmarried man fighting a war, right through to his last ever entry as an eighty-eight-year-old widower, a tired, poorly man fighting a failing heart. Almost a whole life in a large black suitcase. Then there was my mum's few items, the pictures she kept in her room, one of my nan and grandad holding hands in black and white in their drab, old-looking clothes, the clothes that people of that era wore regardless of age. My nan looking older than I do now but in reality years younger as she died aged fifty-six. In my tool bag some of my dad's tools and one of his tobacco tins holding nails and screws instead of the nut-brown tobacco that actually killed him so long ago.

Sometimes I find myself wondering where all the loved ones that have now gone are. Sometimes I momentarily forget and it's almost like they may have just popped out for a while or not phoned for ages. It's like they are still out there, getting on with their lives, doing everyday things. I don't do this consciously, I don't fantasise they are still here, but just at times I am on another plane, an alternate reality where time is suspended, grief is dulled and the merciless actuality of overpowering loss has departed for just a brief moment in time until I am propelled back to the present and the brutal, harsh, overwhelming pain returns and I clutch my chest to try and comfort my aching heart as we all do.

Whether or not this boot sale actually takes place is anyone's guess. It will be ten years in the making if it does happen and also a miracle.

Lastly, we have a mole. It is wreaking havoc on our lawn on both sides which shows it's not fussy about where it wreaks its havoc. Every morning we find new little piles of the finest topsoil you couldn't buy if you tried. We scoop this up and use it, thank you very much, Mr or Mrs Mole, however, we'd prefer it if you'd bugger off and wreak havoc elsewhere, preferably Pembrokeshire or Powys. I am going to try one of these sonar-type deterrents to drive it away; failing that I may play the Susan Boyle CD that was my mum's, and the one item of hers I have no emotional attachment to whatsoever. Knowing our luck the mole will become a big fan of hers and start leaving me requests of what tracks it wants playing whilst it carries on destroying our lawn.

The sun decided to be relentless in its efforts to make my daughters visit a great one. Thank you, sun. Due to its generosity my daughter Louise and I have been able to do most of the things we promised ourselves before her visit.

We started with a couple of trips to the riverside nearby and as we are both wildlife nutters we were never disappointed by the abundant species of insects, reptiles and birds. Louise got to see her first dippers, little brown birds with white chests that dip repeatedly by the side of rivers and streams. So why do dippers dip? There are three theories: One suggests the dipper's repetitive bobbing against a background of turbulent water helps conceal the bird's image from predators. A second asserts that dipping helps it to sight prey beneath the surface of the water, and a third theory is that dipping may be a mode of visual communication among dippers in their very noisy environment coupled with the fact dippers make exaggerated dipping movements during courtship and also to threaten aggressors backs up this particular theory. Whichever it is, the dipper provides an entertaining watch. Kingfishers also flew by us at a speed to rival a space shuttle and makes them almost impossible to photograph. As soon as you see their luminescent blue head coming towards you their orange bum is saying goodbye. I would dearly love to photograph one in flight but dream on, Heather!

We have been to the Royal Botanical Gardens of Wales and seen the butterfly house full of tropical butterflies, some the size of birds.

Their colours are magnificent and breathtaking. The gardens themselves are absolutely beautiful. Lots of walks and a safari around Talley Lakes, getting lost, bitten and worn out. I have to say Louise has been very patient with me hobbling along, some days more than others, and one of her most important tasks is keeping a watch out for other people as I find somewhere to pee! Only time in my life I wish I was male.

In amongst all this the garden and the vegetables needed attention. Helen manned the fort so to speak whilst Lou and I were on our gadabouts. I am amazed how quickly weeds appear. I thought I had done a thorough job one afternoon and had weeded out all the usual suspects, however, within twenty-four hours the weeds had formed a counterattack and had surrounded all the vegetable plants in a standoff. I must admit the veggies show no backbone at all and offer no resistance and to add insult to injury, Edna the Hen has found the vegetable plot and has taken it upon herself to help me out by scratching at the soil and throwing my broccoli seedlings over to the surrounding lawn... How kind of her. Note to self, find a way of stopping Edna before she ends up in a casserole.

We all went to Lampeter today to see some proper shops. Louise foolishly asked if Sainsbury's in Lampeter sold clothes to which I replied, 'No, they barely sell food.' The biggest upset of the day was our unrequited quest for a lemon meringue pie. No luck it seems, so Louise and I have had to make do with Häagen-Dazs Praline and Cream ice cream. I am pleased to announce it satiated our sweet tooth quite well, allaying any disappointments.

Louise could not get over the public transport set up where we live. We can get a bus into Llanfwr on Tuesday but unfortunately we can't get one back until Thursday. The B&Bs do well there.

We have a lot of visitors making their way to Ty Mawr in the coming couple of months and we are looking forward to seeing them all. I am also making my first trip back to England to see my son and his family in Kent, made so much easier by Carol and Steve staying over on their way back from Yorkshire and taking me back with them to East Sussex. Coming back I shall be accompanied by our friend Julie who just so happens to share the same birthdate as me so we shall celebrate it together here.

We are just so lucky to have so many people making the effort to come and see us and hope that they return, and others that have not yet visited can. We are now taking bookings for 2028.

The time Louise was here was over in a flash. The weather was brilliant right up to the day she left when it suddenly became dull and cloudy. We were so lucky and we feel Lou had a really good break. Miss her dreadfully though. She left her mark by creating a stone circle in the garden, fitting in the stones perfectly to form a feature in the centre of our lawn which we have plans for, another project in progress.

As said the weather has now become quite chilly and we have rain. I am happy we have rain because nothing beats a good soaking for the garden and vegetables, however, I really miss the long evenings spent pottering in the fading yet still warm sun. All this has been replaced albeit temporarily with dodging the rainy periods to feed the birds and chickens and water the greenhouse plants, in addition Helen is watching football out of one eye and scrolling on her laptop with the other for more plants! I do not mind and actually do understand the offside rule, and it is always entertaining watching a load of millionaires rolling around on the floor in feigned agony after someone accidentally bumped into them. I would love to see the same men (and I use that term loosely) play rugby. I watched a England women's football match and no-one dived, rolled about on the pitch or wiped non-existent blood from non-existent injuries from their faces or noses. I will leave that there.

CHAPTER 27

I have been poorly lately and I will confess, a right royal pain in the arse. About twelve years ago I went through a period of depression for several reasons culminating in the GP of the time prescribing fluoxetine (Prozac), an SSRI antidepressant. I happily stayed on this for the past twelve years until I decided that given everything in my life now I should come off it. So, I reduced the dose and then stopped. I must mention at this juncture that nurses are probably the worst culprits of not doing what they tell others and stupidly I didn't give it enough time on a lower dose. This has resulted in the worst withdrawal symptoms I have ever experienced. I have mood swings that make Jack Nicholson's character in The Shining look placid. I also have vile headaches, nausea and visual disturbances. It's been two weeks now and I know I am not over the worst, however, if Helen doesn't kill me before then hopefully I will be OK soon. She is currently looking to go back to work full-time in New Zealand. Moral of the story, if you are on fluoxetine or any antidepressant, especially SSRIs, and want to come off, do get medical help. Go to the GP and get a programme of reduction set up to prevent this nightmarish episode in my life. I only write this as a warning to others, it certainly is nothing I am proud of. Hindsight in this case would have been invaluable.

The vegetables are coming into fruition, literally. In the greenhouse, peppers, chillies, cucumbers, tomatoes and salad leaves abound. Outside in the beds, the beans, peas, shallots, garlic, onions, brassicas, kalettes, courgettes and celeriac are all becoming grown-ups and looking good enough to eat. The strawberry bed is literally giving us a punnet a day and I am looking forward to making the strawberry jam for the winter. Our orchard is also starting to bear fruit even though the trees are still very young. In Helen's domain her roses are magnificent – white, peach, red, orange and pink blooms are all around us. She has worked so hard and there are still so many ideas she has to make the garden as she dreams it should look. We interred my mum's ashes in a large blue planter and planted a 'Mum in a Million' rose. It is pink and the fragrance is amazing. She loved the colour pink and whenever I bought her flowers, which I did regularly, they were always pink. I am happy that between us we did this with her remains and wherever I go, she can also go.

We are still only getting one egg a day and Edna is still roving around the garden and digging up the earth in the vegetable beds. She leaves the plants alone so I just rake over the damaged soil and she starts the process all over again, a bit like painting the Forth Bridge, it's never-ending. The other two venture out for a while then settle back into their coop. Gertie lays one egg and that's about the sum of it to date. We are, however, being plagued by jackdaws; these birds have followed me around the country and been the bane of my life everywhere I have lived. We open up the chicken run every morning and every morning the jackdaws descend on the food like a marauding mob devouring every grain and morsel in sight. After doing a bit of research I bought a stuffed fake crow that you lay on its back and its black plastic feet point heavenward to let everyone know it is a deceased crow, a dead crow, it has gone to meet its maker etc., etc. So with this tucked under my arm I marched to the henhouse and positioned it on the grass for all to see, even picking up some of the feathers left behind after the last jackdaw rave and scattering them around to make it look like the fake crow had met a gruesome untimely end. Within minutes, gathered up overhead in the trees dozens of jackdaws were looking on, making a cacophony of noise as if to let all around know one of their comrades had fallen in the line of duty. After about two days of us looking smugly out of our window at the absence of the mob, they returned having worked out old Plastic Feet was a phoney. So we hung it in another place upside down on the advice of Trevor. Didn't work. I could almost hear them laughing at it and pointing with one wing falling off their perches with laughter. I have moved it yet again and it seems to be doing its job but whether or not this will last remains to be seen. Watch this space.

*

Another break in the weather, the rain and wind returned; out came the dogs' dirty paws towel. We actually lit the woodburner one night such was the change in the temperature. The moment Louise left for the sunshine coast the clouds descended and we sat shivering. OK, OK, a slight exaggeration especially as out of nowhere Helen's hot flushes have returned after at least two years and they are enough to provide a heat source for a small country. We blame the return of these sirocco moments on the five years of tamoxifen putting a halt to all the natural progress of those nasty little mind-altering hormones. However, I digress, the sun is back and with a vengeance.

We took our first steps towards becoming beekeepers on Thursday. We went along to one of the East Carmarthen Beekeepers Association meetings and met some lovely people whose knowledge of beekeeping is profound. We observed the bees and the processes that have to be adhered to on hive inspection. One hive had clearly not been provided enough pollen to produce food for the hive and a lot of the bees were very lethargic and some sadly had died. They sprayed the bees with sugar water and within seconds they started to revive. The most amazing spectacle was when the first bees to revive went and collected more of this sugar water and took it to the poorly bees to drink, it was amazing. We have a lot to learn from these remarkable, amazingly industrious insects.

We have now joined the association and will be attending every week working towards a course and then acquisition of our own swarms. Helen was given a hive as a leaving present by her generous and lovely work colleagues when she retired and as two hives are much more beneficial than one solitary hive we will be buying another, along with our outfits etc. We both enjoyed every minute.

Another trip to the Lampeter dump was another highlight of our week; we are going to be on the staff's Christmas card list at this rate – we are by far their best customers. What really is growing more and more cross-making for me is the amount of plastic everything we buy is wrapped up in. We are trying desperately to get everything that doesn't have this toxic crap wrapped around it but there is virtually nothing to be had that is plastic free. The solution is for the world to wake up and find another, environmentally friendly way of presenting products. Most shops here that are independently owned use paper to wrap and paper carrier bags. If I do get my shopping delivered I ask for it not to be put in carrier bags, but then they wrap everything in plastic bags anyway. Why? If we do not wake up soon and do something about this, the planet, especially ocean life, is going to be wiped out. If it wasn't for the human race imagine what a wonderful life the animals and insects and all forms of wildlife would have.

Today was a strange day, talking of wildlife. Phoebe, as has been said before is a predatory dog. She stalks her intended prey and is so quick, if you remember she caught a pheasant and killed it a while back. We have an abundance of fledglings in our garden and most mornings they gather outside and feed before we have let the dogs out. Today unfortunately a fledgling nuthatch fell foul of Phoebe and despite our rescuing it as soon as we could the poor little thing died. We were heartbroken to say the least but fully understand Phoebe has no malice, it's just her nature, but it is so hard not to anthropomorphise and feel some anger towards her. The second occurrence happened later when I went into the conservatory from the garden only to find another nuthatch of all things had flown through the door and was clearly dazed. I picked it up, shaking my head at the incredulity of this happening with the same species of bird on the same day. We sat with it in the garden for a while, willing it to recover and eventually after a long fifteen or so minutes it almost shook its head as if to say, 'Where the hell am I?' and flew away. Helen and I both clapped and cheered.

We also attended the Dinefwr (pronounced Din-ever) Food Festival. This is the deer park Louise and I went to a couple of weeks back. This time it was packed with marquees stuffed with food, chutneys, cheeses, wines, gins, ice cream (a personal favourite), all Welsh produce and it was divine! We bought some blue cheese, chutneys, fruity balsamic vinegar, ciders and a few other items. Needless to say our lunch was superb. We spent the afternoon in our beautiful garden and when I say that it is not to sound proud but grateful, lucky and fortunate. Helen remarked whilst we were at the

Dinefwr that if we had been on holiday we would have been loath to leave the beautiful surroundings of the area, but we have Ty Mawr to come home to and it is equally scenic, and for that we are thankful.

CHAPTER 28

BACKGROUND

Helen and I have been together now for twenty years. It hasn't all be a walk in the park, but we have overcome some major problems along the way.

We met through a lesbian magazine called *Diva*. I put in an advert in the personal column looking for a possible future partner. I had been in a relationship for six years which had been over for quite some time and felt I was ready to look once again to see if I could get it right at last.

My advert was given the title 'Fireside Future' simply because I had said in my introduction, amongst other things, that I liked open fires. If anyone was interested they would leave a message on a dedicated phone voicemail that I accessed with a PIN number. Several women had responded and I gainly listened and spoke with many, actually meeting some for a drink but no sparks were produced. I lived in Suffolk at this point working as a staff nurse in an NHS general hospital. I lived alone in a semi-rural part of the county and was reasonably content but did feel I would like a girlfriend to share it all with.

Eventually I listened to a message from someone who introduced herself as Helen, softly spoken and unassuming. I rang her and we arranged to meet. As she lived in London I suggested halfway but at this point Helen was in a job that called for her to travel extensively and she knew the nearest town to where I lived well and insisted we meet there in a pub car park at midday.

By now I have to admit I was becoming jaded with this blind dating set-up and I went along without much enthusiasm, expecting very little in the way of success of meeting someone I gelled with and wanted to see again.

I sat in the pub car park under an archway listening to the car radio as I was early. Helen had told me her car was white and also the make and model so when she appeared I knew instantly she had arrived. First thoughts? She looks nice. Now 'nice' is an innocuous word really, but that was the first word that my brain came up with. We both got out of our cars and shook hands and made our way over to the pub to have lunch.

Conversation flowed easily. We spoke about where we live, past relationships and what things we loved and disliked. We found we were very similar in outlook, both into photography, wildlife and avid readers of books. After lunch we wandered around the town and visited an antiques market and it seemed like we had known each other a lot longer than two hours or so.

When it was time to go Helen asked if we could see each other again and I readily agreed and after some phone conversations and making various arrangements I visited her in London and basically the rest is history. We didn't live together for about three years but did spend a lot of time in each other's homes, weekends and holidays.

During our early years Helen decided on a career change and wanted to go to university to study podiatry. This was a lifelong wish of hers and I encouraged her to apply and she was accepted at the University of Brighton and with that I was lucky enough to secure a nursing post in the area and we found a house and started to live together in earnest.

They were strange times; Helen was working flat out to obtain her degree and I embarked on mine in district nursing, so at one point we were both writing dissertations. In addition to this we had moved yet again to accommodate my mum who was becoming frail and needed help with her personal needs and meals etc., and along the way we had acquired three boxer dogs – George, Lily and Maisie – so our little household was growing.

Degrees passed, we both started new jobs, me in Brighton and Helen in Worthing. Helen's sister Daphne was living in Spain at the time in a very unhappy marriage. She came to visit us one summer and never went back to Spain except to collect her belongings and arrange furniture removals. I managed to find her a job where I worked in administration and we continued all living together. At one point my eldest son also lived there for a while whilst studying for his MSc.

Gradually as time went on, Daphne moved in with her dad who was becoming frailer with age and we looked around for a house in the country. We found one, a beautiful Victorian farmhouse inland and nearer to where Helen worked. We had lovely time there and this was the catalyst for us to eventually want to live in the countryside.

In 2011 Helen had what she thought was lump in her right breast. She is the last person to go to the GP for anything. I have to nag tirelessly before she will go but I was concerned when she went without prompting. She was sent for a scan and remarkably the cancerous tumour was in the left breast. Someone was watching over her! Fortunately it was caught early and she underwent surgical removal and radiotherapy for twelve weeks plus the five-year tamoxifen plan. She now has the all clear.

In November 2012 Helen's sister Daphne, who had retired in the October, went on a Slimming World diet and phoned me one day to say that her stomach wasn't getting smaller at all and if anything was getting bigger. She had complained on and off for the last year or so about discomfort there and had also visited her GP several times and was fobbed off with pills and more pills, most of her symptoms being blamed on irritable bowel. However, this time the GP sent her for a scan and that's when the awful truth was revealed. She had Primary Peritoneal Cancer, PPC, rare with a low survival rate.

It was decided that she would come and live with us as their dad was coping reasonably well, so we could look after her during her chemotherapy and any post-operation recovery periods. Her medical notes were transferred to East Sussex and in the February she started her treatment. At first it appeared the chemotherapy was working but this was short-lived and by the July she was given months to live. Daphne was stoic and never complained. I could tell by Helen's reaction to it all that she was in complete denial. As a nurse and one that had vast experience of terminal care I knew the signs. A lot of the team looking after her were my colleagues and friends and thus more of an insight than most.

During this dreadful time George the boxer fell foul to cancer too and the day Daphne was given her terminal prognosis we had George euthanised. Ten weeks late Lily the boxer was struck blind by a cranial cancer and she too was euthanised. We felt under attack. This growing family around us suddenly started to diminish and it's finality made our heads spin.

By September we had installed a hospital bed into the living room so Daphne could gaze out of the window onto the countryside around us which she did frequently. The district nursing team and the Macmillan nurses all known to me professionally were as usual magnificent.

During the last throws of an Indian summer in late September one afternoon after lunch Daphne took herself to her bed and fell asleep. After trying to rouse her we realised this was her last hours on earth and both of us sat either side of the bed holding a hand each. It was a balmy night and we could hear the owls hooting outside and the sound of night-time insects as we watched every breath she took until she took no more. She was sixty-four.

I'm not sure how we picked ourselves up from that and I am not sure we have. I was diagnosed with rheumatoid arthritis within a week after Daphne's death. My hands and feet had swollen and become inflamed and then the rest of my joints not wanting to be left out, joined in. My mother started to show signs of dementia and was diagnosed with vascular dementia with paranoia, months after. Helen's dad, following Daphne's death became very frail and had stopped caring for himself. And after visiting him Helen brought him home to us and it was decided we would have to sell his house and find a house nearer to Helen's work and preferably a bungalow, as neither my mum nor her dad could manage stairs anymore.

We moved to a chalet bungalow in Worthing and I hated it. It had a small garden, and although it was a nice house, it just didn't feel like home at all. My mum's health declined rapidly, to the point where I couldn't leave her at all. Even if I hung the washing out I had a baby alarm attached to me so I could hear her if she tried to get up or fall. She did fall, with monotonous regularity, fortunately not hurting herself. In the end I was exhausted. I phoned Adult Social Care to see what help I was entitled to and after a visit from the social worker and a mental health assessment it was arranged that Mum would go into a home for some respite care.

When I took my mum to the home I thought my heart would break and never, ever, recover and I was right. I have never forgiven myself for letting her go, although the home was wonderful, better than I could have wished, and the members of staff will remain very dear to me as friends now, but at the time, it was a dreadful period of my life.

Helen's father had heart failure and it was heartbreaking to see him struggle every day to do the simplest of tasks. He never dressed in the end but was content to sit in his dressing gown and pyjamas. Helen took care of his personal hygiene but even the effort of a shower once a week was overwhelming. Slowly and surely his health declined and there was no doubt in either of our minds that he could not go on much longer and more importantly he didn't want to. He was a man of strong faith and confided in me that he prayed daily to be taken. His wish came true one afternoon in September and his funeral was held on the same date as Daphne's and by coincidence, Helen's mother's birthday. As Helen said, that day was a real family occasion.

So that left just the two of us and our old dog Maisie, a boxer of ten years who had already been through cancer treatment. The following year she left us also and the house seemed like an empty chasm where once it was filled with family. We got Flo within a week; we were well aware she would not replace Maisie but we needed some joy in our lives and Flo did just that. She was such a confident little puppy. The first thing she did after the journey back from picking her up from the breeder was to grab my kitchen broom and take it into the living room and chew! She wasn't in the least stressed by the separation or her new surroundings.

It was obvious after few weeks that Flo was bored witless with my company and was so playful she needed a friend. We decided to rescue a dog from Greece where a wonderful woman runs a dog and cat rescue for all the abandoned animals on Zante. She is an angel. Our good friends had already rescued from her and so we asked for a young dog that could deal with a boxer puppy and she came up with Phoebe. Phoebe is white and orange, a bit like a pointer or foxhound but of unknown genetic makeup! They took to each other immediately and we have never looked back. They play all day, sleep together, eat together and Phoebe tolerates Flo stealing her toys and bones without fuss.

We holidayed in Wales every year as we both loved the country, its mountains, hills, never-ending landscape of greens and browns full of trees, lakes, rivers and forests. We knew that our move could prove unpopular with family and friends and the worst thing would be leaving my mum in the home. I spoke with the manager and staff and I was assured she would be fine. She was very happy and I had to remind her most visits who I was. The plan was to visit her once a month and FaceTime with her in-between thanks to the deputy manager offering to use her mobile phone. I convinced myself we could do it and everyone around me said it was our time to have some happiness. So the house went on the market in the March and by the July we had sold it. The house we had set our heart on fell through, as did another, and in the September we once again went back to Wales and found this cottage.

We were due to move early December and as the time approached I spent as much time as I could visiting Mum, feeling nothing but guilt. One Saturday night three weeks before we were due to go I received a phone call from the care home informing me that Mum had fallen out of bed and an ambulance had been called. On arrival at the home I found Mum black and blue and completely disorientated. She had a massive swelling on her head, with bruising to her face and arm. It was devastating to see.

It was established she had suffered a haemorrhage to her brain either due to the fall or before and the fall was a result of the bleed; she had also developed pneumonia. After a few days it was clear she was terminally ill and arrangements to get her back to the home were made. Mum died with Helen and I with her two days later in the home that cared for her so well.

Her funeral was held four days before we moved.

Looking back on this I do wonder how we managed to overcome so much loss and heartache but I am sure if you were to delve into anyone's past there will always be sadness and loss, and we all have to somehow just carry on. So carry on we do.

CHAPTER 29

As if to prove a point regarding other people's lives:

Having gone through depression myself and the subsequent horrors of coming off the antidepressants recently (I must stress that this was entirely my own fault for not getting proper advice), this week highlighted just how bad mental health illness can get.

My grandson Jack, aged twenty-one, lost one of his oldest friends to mental health problems. This friend of the same age was a talented musician, artist and going by the Facebook tributes a really nice guy. I remember a bespectacled happy boy that came to Jack's parties and his lovely parents who my daughter became friends with. This lovely man ended his life without any hint of a problem by jumping off Beachy Head. I can only imagine and not do justice to the pain his mum and dad and sisters must be going through. I shake my head in disbelief; goodness only knows what his family are doing. I have always said that if we have anything malfunction physically we do not hesitate to visit our GP, our friends and family sympathise and wish us well, they empathise with our broken leg, arthritis, colds or flu, even a toothache draws remarks such as, 'That's horrible,' or, 'There is nothing worse.' Well there is plenty worse both physically and mentally. In this example the brain, the most important organ we possess, the one that controls everything we do and feel, when that malfunctions it appears there are still taboos around this subject and very little empathy and understanding.

I'm not sure why, we as humans cannot respond appropriately. Is it either we simply do not understand or have very little sympathy, or are scared? Phrases such as 'it's all in the mind' or 'snap out of it' or 'you need a hobby' are bandied around flippantly until the sufferer begins to feel that they are malingerers or a burden or worse. This tragic outcome, whatever the reason, knocked me for six this week. Some mental health problems are as terminal as some cancers and until as much research, resources and understanding goes into this problem as is apportioned to cancer and other diseases, it will just continue and other families will have to suffer the same devastating fate as this young man's parents and family.

I had some time on my own for the last few days as Helen went to Sussex to catch up with work colleagues. I got lonely, I must admit. I am content in my own company usually but I think given the news I had and my ongoing withdrawal symptoms I have found it hard being on my own. The dogs are a blessing; they are constant companions, so much so that I am stepping over them, tripping over them and negotiating my way down our stairs to try and avoid them and not find myself at the bottom before I anticipated!

The heatwave, as it is officially declared, has found me watering the garden for at least an hour every night to ensure the vegetables are not fried to a crisp under the unrelenting sun. I do enjoy this and it is a necessity but after the first thirty minutes it becomes a bit tiresome. However, I will soon be moaning about the rain and longing for the sunshine again. This has been a treat, having this heatwave, especially after all the warnings we had about the Welsh weather. However, I am well aware the rest of the country has been having the same. It has been far too hot to work properly in the garden, just pottering in-between sitting in the shade and taking it easy, most of our gardening is getting done after seven in the evening.

Tonight we were treated to a firefly display outside our front door. They were streaming toward the outside lights and as we watched they left a trail of light in their ever-increasing activities. Some darting across, some just turning circles. A whole mayhem of tiny flashes and streams of light caused by the female in her attempt to attract a mate. They are actually beetles, not flies, but I have never seen anything like it before. What another treat to add to the ever-growing list of firsts here are Ty Mawr.

We had our gate mended today by Dai the builder. Dai is a seventy-plus, thin, wiry man who looks as though he hasn't got long on this earth but actually his looks bely the physical strength he actually possesses. We had to replace the post on the farm gate at the front of our drive which became damaged by a van driver reversing into it. Fortunately we had one in the dovecote going spare, as you do. These are massively heavy but he dragged it over to the gate like a matchstick. The heavy farm gate was blocking exit on our drive and Helen needed to go out to get Dai his cash as everything is cash around here. I asked Dai to give me a hand but unfortunately I lost grip on the gate and it crashed down on two fingers of my left hand, causing a crush injury right across one nail and the first joint of the other. This coupled with my RA was excruciating and Helen walked past me to go to the car oblivious to my plight. She caught sight of my hand and then my face and we went back into the house. I nearly passed out with the pain, I kid you not! Our first reaction was cold water but to be honest warm was far more soothing. My mum always said heat draws the pain. Once again, Mother knows best.

*

The weather here is almost tropical! Evidently temperatures have broken records in Wales and even the river near our house can be walked across with ease now. I am not complaining but some rain would be good before the whole of the UK is on a hosepipe ban and the landscape resembles the outbacks of Australia. Personally I get exhausted in this heat, Helen swears it's the RA as her mum could never cope with it. I have to say my joints are particularly bad at present. I can't work in it either and any work needed doing waits until the evening. However, as said previously, before we know it we will all be reaching for the gloves and scarves and wishing it was summer again.

I'm not a huge football fan and don't profess to be an expert in any shape or form but I am enjoying this World Cup, especially now England are through to the semi-finals. I love the management style of the unassuming Gareth Southgate and the way he appears to have a well-managed, disciplined team. They don't roll around dying because someone looked at them the wrong way and they are actually playing good football. They kept their cool under the awful tactics of

Columbia, which shows they are a well-structured bunch of men. Good for them; for the first time in a long time I look forward to an England game where I am not expecting them to lose! What an achievement it would be if we actually do win this cup. Arise, Sir Gareth?

We haven't really been up to much given this weather. The dogs are content to just lie underneath the large silver willow we have in the centre of our front piece of garden. Underneath it we have a niger seed feeder and the siskins and goldfinches are numerous, all vying for a place on it, so we installed two more which are equally popular. The amount of bird feeders we have are many, but the pleasure we glean from feeding them and watching them is invaluable. As we have large bushes growing along our borders we also have dozens of house sparrows that congregate in them. It is quite amazing to see this synchronised take-off and landing. One minute you can be staring at an empty shrub and before you can blink a host of sparrows all land in it and apart from the chirping you wouldn't know they were in there such is their camouflage. When we first moved here the constant whistling of the red kites made us look up in anticipation of catching sight of this glorious bird that soars above, in some instances quite low looking for prey. Now we have become quite used to it and although its mewing sound does still raise our eyes skywards after the first few calls, it is so commonplace to us now. Strange, isn't it? I remember one holiday in Wales not so long ago when Helen and I got in the car in search of finding one, desperate to catch a glimpse, now they fly overhead with barely a glance. We promise ourselves we won't take things for granted and in a way we don't but familiarity does breed if not contempt certainly some apathy.

The greenhouse is full of tomato, cucumber, pepper and chilli plants and the temperature in there is phenomenal, so much so I have taken some plants out as they couldn't cope! Runner beans and French beans are climbing like crazy and we will no doubt have courgettes coming out of our ears! On the other hand the brassica plants are plagued by the dreaded cabbage white butterfly and the other day I took off at least twenty caterpillars despite the netting I put up. Helen added another layer of this and so far it seems to be working but I am not holding out much hope for a bumper crop of greens and the like. The chickens are all roaming free, no more sitting around in their house, however, this has not proved to make them productive egg-wise as we are now getting no eggs whatsoever. They just get up, go outside, peck and scratch around, even into the neighbouring field, and then come home and go back to bed again, adding nothing to the upkeep of the home at all... Adolescent chickens?

Helen attended the first part of an intensive beekeeping course last Saturday and thoroughly enjoyed it. The people that run it are known to us now as we have been going to the apiary every week to observe and help where we can. Due to this weather the honey production is amazing. When the boards were being lifted out of the hive the honey was just dripping off. The bees were not happy this week, however, they were making their disapproval of our interference in their hive very evident, even stinging me through a rubber glove. Helen and I both had our beekeeping suits now and so glad of it, but it is not a hobby to be entered into lightly and we are both so grateful for the help and support we know we will be getting. Hopefully this time next year we will have our first swarm and honey will be forthcoming.

CHAPTER 30

The unrelenting fine weather continues and after a visit to our local nursery yesterday and arriving home with new plants to put in our borders, we realised we would need a jackhammer to dig the ground up to get them in! We stared at the cracked brown terra firma beneath us and decided a fork would have to do in the absence of a JCB digger. Helen gritted her teeth and managed to dig a hole deep enough to place the plants in. She is a genius with a fork, that woman.

I have probably mentioned before that Phoebe, our little Greek rescue is part pointer, part git. She stalks everything – bees, wasps, butterflies, birds, you name it, Phoebe sees it as potential prey and the posture straight away goes into the doggie equivalent of the Ministry of Silly Walks. The tail goes out straight, the nose is pushed forwards and then the daft walk begins. Slowly and surely one paw after another she edges her way towards her intended prey. Most of the time Flo sits there watching her, a bored look on her face, then just as Phobe is ready to pounce, up leaps Flo and spoils the whole thing with the intended victim flying off frantically and Pheebs left staring at the space it once occupied. However, there are occasions when Flo is otherwise engaged in digging a hole in the lawn, chewing a stolen plastic flower pot or trying to scrounge food from us that leave Phoebe to stalk undisturbed. In these instances she has been unfortunately successful in catching whatever it is and the final straw came with the fledgling nuthatch's demise. So Phoebe is now the proud owner of a bell hanging off her collar. It jingles continuously when she is prowling around and therefore alerts everything within hearing distance to her presence. It is driving us nuts as it sounds as though there is a permanent ice-cream van driving up and down our little lane, but the wildlife are grateful even if Helen and I are on our way to a nervous breakdown.

The estate we live on used to be owned by posh people. There is a derelict mansion in the near distance that has gone to rack and ruins literally and this was once owned by gentry and has seen grander times. From our garden we can see what is left of magnificent chimneys and a large terrace. I can almost see ladies on the terrace sipping from champagne glasses dressed in their finery when the house was at its finest. The residences that are now occupied were a variety of coach houses, barns and tied cottages all converted into contemporary living spaces and all Grade II listed. The estate dates back to circa 1600 and we were given a large book on estate by the previous owners of Ty Mawr. I must admit I haven't read it yet but have browsed it and picked out some interesting bits and pieces. In all there are about half a dozen residences occupied on the estate, and the actual estate is geared toward fishing and the despicable practice of pheasant shoots.

The reason I mention this potted history of our estate is because we have a new neighbour. When I say neighbour, her home which was a coach house is just visible from our garden. Her name is Christine and she seems quite pleasant. The coach house has stood empty for quite a time so she has a challenge ahead of her. Trevor, the resident nice bloke and friend to all, has once again stepped in and helped her no end. Yesterday Dai the aged, half-dead builder/plasterer/you name it he does it, turned up to cut down three trees which were overgrown and evidently blocking out a lot of natural light. I hate seeing trees destroyed and we both felt really sad to see them drop one by one. Trevor worked tirelessly to help Dai who hasn't been out of hospital long with pancreatitis, ensuring the job got done and to ensure Dai didn't overdo things in this searing heat. At one point Trevor said that Dai nearly ended up head first into the industrial shredder they had hired.

'He dived in like fucking Superman, bud,' he told us. 'I thought he was a fucking goner!'

Sometimes if you leave out the expletives with Trevor he says very little. Evidently Trevor grabbed Dai by the legs to stop him ending up resembling a scene from the film A Texas Chainsaw Massacre.

So we shall see what our new neighbour brings to this small hamlet. I'm quite sure this summer will see a get-together of all of us one evening to welcome her here, and if anyone can make you feel welcome it is Trevor.

We have to go to Swansea tomorrow to have breast scans; we have an appointment fifteen minutes apart. We both, like most of the female population, are not exactly looking forward to having each breast squashed flat for an excruciating sixty seconds or so but this procedure saves lives and by my reckoning it will be the last one I am offered. Helen's of course is crucial given her history so it is a necessary evil, and if you haven't gone for yours when you have been called then make an appointment today, if you are female of course. We lost a very dear friend Marriane two years ago to breast cancer, which hit us both hard as Helen and Marriane went through their treatment at the same time, at one point and called themselves the Tamoxifen Twins. So hopefully all will be well but health is something not to be taken for granted.

Helen as I type, has got the right hump with me as evidently I have eaten her aniseed rock she brought home from her last visit to Worthing. She plonked two rocks on our kitchen table when she was unpacking and said, 'There we are, the rocks you asked for.'

So I took her at her word and ate them both, being the pig that I am, and a sucker for aniseed. I am now in the doghouse and no offer of any substitution from me is rocking her boat.

To be perfectly honest there has been a lull in proceedings here at Ty Mawr. The sunshine continues although we did have a heavy downpour the other day for about forty minutes but since then the dry spell goes on.

We watched England leave the World Cup and personally I think they did so well to get where they did. So good on them. Wimbledon turned out to be its usual predictable self but the tennis was amazing. We managed to see some matches in-between our attempts to keep on top of the garden and household chores.

Our vegetable garden seems to be overtaken by courgettes. I only planted four plants out of the seeds I grew and they have turned into triffids planning world domination. Everything has decided to grow, thank goodness, and slowly but surely we are beginning to harvest the benefits. It's been a good trial run as I have been able to work out what should go where and what is best to grow for next year but as it is our first season all in all we have done well. Even the chickens have started laying again which is a relief. We think they had a moult, which stopped them laying as they need the protein to produce new feathers. We kept finding feathers everywhere and one of the hens looked really tatty so hopefully that was all the problem was.

Helen and I tackled the dry stream bed and sides. Where the water used to be an abundance, weeds and grasses made their appearance and the whole thing started to look really unkempt but the more we stared at it the less we wanted to sort it out. Finally from somewhere we found the energy and I got the petrol strimmer out and Helen had her trusty scythe and between us made it look much better. I looked like something out of Transformers with the harness for the strimmer on both shoulders, the protective eyewear and gloves striding into the jungle of plant life that covered every inch of the stream bed and sides. Needless to say when we had finished we were both completely knackered and the next day even blinking was an effort but it's done and we have sworn never to let it get that overgrown again.

We have loads of sheep again in the adjoining field; they have all been shorn of their thick woolly coats and that must be such a relief for them in this weather. It's really strange but you get really used to their constant bleating and can distinguish the adult calls from the lambs. Like in humans the adult sheep's bleat is low and deep whereas the lambs have a high-pitched voice which does resemble a baby's cry at times. Neither of the dogs are bothered by them now, except at times Flo becomes curious if they gather near our fence and the other day she was nose-to-nose with an adult sheep, both of them eyeing each other with mutual respect. Nothing came of the encounter, both just wandering off in their own direction after it but it was quite touching to see both animals 'having a moment'.

Awaiting now the arrival tomorrow of Carol and Steve who are making their way down the country from the Isle of Berneray after their holiday and picking me up on the way to whizz me off to theirs for a few days, then onto my son's for a further few days and then an overnight stop in Worthing, and back here again with Jenny. It will be lovely to spend some time with the family and I know the cottage and gardens are in very good hands with Helen at the helm. It will be strange though, to be back in the real world again.

*

Well, I am back! I had a lovely time being thoroughly spoilt by Carol and Steve and Ann and Steve. It was lovely to see them all and I hope they enjoyed seeing me too. The first few days were spent at Carol and Stuart's. I caught up with Louise and Jack for a meal and it was lovely to see them both again. Back at Carol's we all went out for lovely Chinese meal in Brighton. It was enlightening to be back in the real world for a few days. It's a strange feeling really because the traffic, the crowds, the shops and the general hustle and bustle were all so familiar to me but I could not help thinking how peaceful Ty Mawr and our surroundings are in comparison. It almost felt like an onslaught to my senses after eight months in Wales. Don't get me wrong, as I looked around at all the people having fun, skateboarding, cycling, driving with their music reverberating the ground underneath us or just generally being weird, it was fun and Brighton at its best. It was great to be there amongst it all but I prefer what we have now. I guess I am just a retired old lady now living in a cottage in the country. Should I change my name to Miss Marple?

The second part of my time away was spent with my son David and his wife Ann and of course the two beautiful granddaughters Emily and Esther. It was just lovely to be with them all, laughing and chatting and generally just chilling. They have a beautiful home which they have both worked for so hard and the girls are a delight.

The journey home was eventful as trains were cancelled; actually one train was cancelled… mine. So an hour journey back to East Sussex was to take two and a half hours, however, thanks to my two superheroes Carol and Steve I was picked up at St Leonard's, saving me schlepping my way over to Eastbourne from there. After a short stay I was then taken to Jenny's for the night and we travelled back here together via the National Express coach from Gatwick which took in all seven hours of chugging along, bumping all the way. Have you ever tried to use a loo on one of these? I found it impossible, ending up in urinary retention until I got home! I now have the bladder muscles of a sixteen-year-old. What a workout!

So home. I woke up this morning to the sound of birds, kites and sheep. Believe it or not there was a reasonable dew on the grass which is why I think our grass is still green mostly. The vegetables have gone bonkers. I found hiding underneath the courgette greenery massive marrows that could have been courgettes about a week ago. As I searched through the greenery, they all laid in the earth like the pods that were everywhere in the film Alien. Needless to say I am now working out how many ways I can use them in chutneys, jams and recipes for meals. I have a feeling Helen and I may get a little tired of this diet.

CHAPTER 31

So the rain has come in abundance bringing with it, here at least, hailstones the size of marbles! At one point it was so bad the dogs fled from the conservatory in fear; the noise was deafening as it splattered ferociously onto the polycarbonate roof. I literally could not hear myself speak.

Needless to say the daily watering of produce and the like has not been necessary. The chickens are not keen either and are staying firmly in their house, only venturing out in-between showers. A bit like us, really. However, we did venture out last night...

There is a community-run pub/restaurant/shop/post office in Colbran which I have mentioned we have dined in before. It's an experience we like to share with our visitors where possible as the whole place was under threat of closure and the local villagers stepped in and bailed it out both financially and by employing themselves to run it. Every Saturday someone takes it in turn to cook and the menu although limited offers two selections of starters, main and dessert. The restaurant and bar are tiny, seating about seventeen people in the dining room area, and the actual bar would be crammed to capacity with half a dozen people in it. The building does extend upstairs where two sitting rooms with books and the loos are. So we decided to treat Jenny to a meal there for her to acquaint herself with the local environment and culture. We arrived after having booked our table for three in good time before seven and were ushered upstairs into the 'living room'. The 'living room' consisted of a room about fifteen feet by twelve feet. Two bookcases stood drunkenly on the walls crammed with old books that were free to anyone to read and return. There were two large sofas covered in crochet blankets and on the floor were piles of old boxes of games and various other items strewn about. In the centre was our table situated in front of a cast-iron fireplace with four fairy lights hanging over logs and newspaper in an attempt to add ambience.

The actual bar downstairs only has room for one bartender and there are no pumps, just bottles and if you're lucky the drink you want is either in stock or in the fridge. In our case it was neither but we soldiered on. On the menu that night to start with was salmon puff or mozzarella puff, followed by what can only be described as indescribable. It was a sort of cabbage, mozzarella-type dish with a whole yolk of an egg in the centre served with peas and new potatoes. I am not the fussiest of eaters and neither is Helen but neither of us felt we had experienced a gastronomic orgasm. Jenny seemed to enjoy hers though so maybe it's us? The dessert was a summer pudding which was actually tasty..

Jenny has proved to be a very easy house guest and is enjoying her relaxed stay here. Both of us share the same birthday next week so we are in the process of trying to decide what form this momentous day should take in the way of celebration. When I was with Carol and Steve I was treated on my first night there to fish and chips, something I had not tasted for at least eight months and since then I have found my mind wandering back, wishing I could have it all over again. I have found a fish and chip restaurant with good reviews in Llanfwr and I would love to go there for another fish and chip supper, however, watch this space as it could all change.

I actually do feel slightly chilly and last night my flip-flops were abandoned for my slippers. This season has brought about some really odd weather. On our journey here we saw yellow, dried-out grass fields all over the place where the lack of rain has beaten the once green landscape into submission. Wales seemed to be more green than England and I am guessing it may be because of the prevailing Atlantic weather that hits us first. Well, actually Ireland first which is even greener than Wales, hence the name 'Emerald Isle'.

This coming week we have no firm plans, it all really depends on the weather. I did enjoy the heatwave I have to confess, but it is nice to have the respite from the heat for a while, however, if the sun is listening, it's OK to come back now.

It's the season for us to be able to welcome all of the visitors we have coming to see us in the coming weeks.

Jenny stayed with us for a double celebration of our birthdays; both Jenny and I celebrate our birthdays on the 2nd August. We spent a lovely morning at Dinefwr Country Park, seeing the deer albeit at a distance and then looking at the exhibition they had there about life below stairs. Interesting and astounding the amount of hours they worked and the number of chores they had to perform in that given time. What a life they had to lead. We don't really know we have been born.

Next up Jean and Jazz came for the day Saturday, and they are too thinking about coming to live in Wales and picked our brains about the pros and cons of leaving 'civilisation' and living in the wilds of Wales. I think we have convinced them that it is worth the leap of faith it takes to make that move. We do not regret a moment of it. I only have to look out of any window and see the plethora of birds that fly in and out of the hedgerows in our garden, the rolling hills that surround us and the thick green pine forest visible from our front door and living room windows to know we have chosen the right course. The dogs roam free around the garden for most of the day, only coming in when they are hot, thirsty or hungry or in Phoebe's case when she spots something to manically bark at and is herded indoors until she calms down, Flo following in her wake, clueless.

Due to the rainfall of late our grass is lush and green again and everything has picked up once more and returned to its former glory. Amazing how quickly nature recovers and carries on where it left off before it is stricken with whatever the elements throw at it. My greenhouse is overflowing with peppers, chillies, cucumbers and green tomatoes and the hens have decided that they like it in there and I have to oust them out frequently. All along the floor of the greenhouse are little dustbowls they have made to sit in and I spend most of my time raking it over to level it again. We are still only getting an egg a day and I am beginning to think we have been quite unlucky with these hens as they are entirely fussy eaters. They will not touch the Layers Pellets which is their staple diet. They refuse any scraps we give them (except for the spaghetti) and even the corn mix gets ignored. I have checked them over for any signs of mites and other problems that chickens get but I am scratching my head over why we have pernickety chickens. I do think that animals see Helen and I as gullible idiots, knowing we will do our utmost to make their lives a good one, but everyone else I speak to who keeps chickens or has in the past tells me how they eat anything. What are we doing wrong? Any suggestions?

So next week we have three friends of Helen's coming to visit and staying for a week, really hoping the sun shines for us all. We are actually booked up until the end of October now. Both Helen and I feel so flattered people want to come and stay with us and we also feel so grateful we are able to share this little piece of peace and quiet with them. I am pleased to say that everyone who visits leaves feeling rested and relaxed. Job done!

Tomorrow we are having a BBQ in the garden with all of the neighbours – the last of the birthday celebrations. It is always a good laugh and fun to get together and never do we end the evening without promises of produce, offers of help with certain projects or ideas or solutions to any issues to do with the garden or house etc. It is like a very small commune and we all look out for one another here. No-one goes into town without ensuring no-one else needs anything. Any surplus produce or seedlings are shared around and Trevor always brings me eggs when he wants another sponge cake made… 'You don't have to cook it today, tomorrow will do.' This is always said with his usual bare-faced cheek and a wink of an eye. How could I say no when this man would do absolutely anything if you asked him? He finds great delight though in winding Helen up. He will tell her stories with a deadpan face all the while winking at me to let me in on the joke and poor Helen, not wishing to contradict him gets lured into believing him, such is the sincerity of his face and voice. Finally he breaks into a grin and the penny drops and we all collapse in fits of laughter.

There is not a time of day we do not like here either. The early mornings are full of birdsong, bleating lambs and cockerels crowing to herald the new day. The mornings bring the usual round of chores before the relative peace of the afternoon where we can choose to relax or carry on gardening and the like. Our evenings can be filled if we choose with sitting in the dying light of the sun watching the incredible unpolluted skyline turn from inky blue to black and sparkle around the waxing and waning moon. On a good night you can clearly see Mars and Saturn in the night sky with the aid of a night sky app I have on my phone which locates your position and lets you know what is above you. It shows satellites also which always amazes me as to the numbers of them there are, floating above us. The sky is so busy and abundant with so many stars and planets. The old adage about feeling so infinitesimal in comparison always comes to my mind as I gaze in wonder at this sight and then to bed to do it all over again the next day.

CHAPTER 32

Standing by the greenhouse looking at the abundance of green tomatoes, peppers and cucumbers, I heard this strange squeaky noise coming from the other side of the now dried-up stream. At first I thought the chickens were distressed or having a disagreement so I decided to investigate. After a short while there was movement in the bank and at first I thought it was a rat. I sighed because rats can be one hell of a problem especially to chickens but on second glance I realised it was what I thought was a stoat. I have since found out they were weasels. I called Helen over and we sat and watched in wonder at these tiny little creatures scurrying around a small area on the stream bank and popping in and out of holes that we always suspected were occupied by something. Helen managed to get our cameras and we were able to take some close-up shots. I have never seen a weasel before and to have them in our garden was a real treat. It made us feel so lucky to be able to experience wildlife at its purest and its best.

We have had such a busy couple of days. Our BBQ went very well and we all enjoyed the afternoon. There was lots of food, drink and good banter and we chatted long into the evening, watching the sun go down. In the darkness tawny owls hooted, young barn owls screeched in the background awaiting their parents' return with food, bats flew overhead and in the distance sheep bleated, breaking the absolute silence of the night-time here at Ty Mawr.

The next morning Helen and I decided it was time to catch up on long overdue chores. The brassicas have taken a battering from the cabbage white butterflies and we had put up some netting to try and stop them but it was a bit slapdash and so we decided to erect frames and have the correct netting in place. We are pleased with the results and the butterflies have seemingly given up and gone to Trevor and Catherine's, according to them. Weeding was done, marmalade was made, runner beans blanched and frozen along with other vegetables. I am still looking at the pile of marrows we have, at a loss at what to do. There are only so many you can eat although the marrows and ginger jam will be made soon so that should use up some. Once the tomatoes ripen I shall be making all sorts of sauces and chutneys and have decided that shelving needs to go up in the garage to cater for the jars of preserves that will soon need home as our pantry is already full.

Trevor is cutting down load of ash trees that have been stricken with ash dieback disease and hired Dai to help him. I may have mentioned before that Dai is a very frail-looking elderly gentleman who looks like he should be in a bath chair with a blanket over his knees, not wielding a chainsaw halfway up a tree. Sometime this afternoon Trevor came over to us asking for painkillers.

'What's wrong then?' I asked, rummaging through the cupboard trying to find something.

'Nothing with me,' Trevor said. 'It's Dai, he has a pain down his left arm and he's gone a funny colour.' I immediately stopped looking for the pills and turned around to face him.

'What colour?' I said, my suspicions aroused as to whether Dai was having a heart attack.

'Fucking purple,' Trevor responded. 'I thought he was going to drop.' I decided the best bet was for me to go and look at purple Dai myself but Trevor insisted he was fine and said matter-of-factly, 'If he drops he drops.' So ibuprofen in hand he marched off up the lane. We could hear the constant noise of the chainsaw but when it stopped for any length of time Helen and I looked at each other wondering if Dai had 'dropped'.

Trevor arrived again tonight to help us dust the hens for red mite. 'Was Dai OK in the end?' I asked.

'Aye, bud, the pills took the pain off but it was back again after a couple of hours. I thought he was a goner but he is back in the morning as we haven't finished.'

The chickens didn't seem to enjoy being hung upside down and having their armpits (or should I say wing pits?) doused with powder, but we have done this a precaution just in case they have red mites. Trevor held each one upside down and I doused, getting it on Trevor as I did so. He grabbed a handful and put it under his armpits and then his crotch and said, 'You can never be too careful,' and then carried on with the job. He never fails to make us laugh, that man.

We have our friends coming tomorrow; Helen is picking them up from Swansea bus station but unfortunately the weather looks like it is on course for rain so we shall have to see what the days bring us as to what our plans are. I am sure whatever the weather we shall have a relaxing time.

We haven't chosen the easy life here at Ty Mawr, quite the opposite, but to be perfectly honest the thought of retirement with nothing to do wouldn't suit us. I think a lot of retired people find they now have time to pursue the hobbies and lifestyle they have always thought about leading and whatever it is they fill their days amply. There are some evenings when both of us are pleased the day is drawing to end so we can sit and lapse into a coma but I wouldn't change our lives for the world.

However, I am moaning that it is raining too much and I long for the hot, sultry, humid days that were July. Uncomfortable, yes, too hot, yes, but so lovely to go out in and see the activity of the insects on the flowers and plants, the butterflies rejoicing in the sunshine and the birds savouring every moment of knowing they would survive the night without losing too much body heat. On the plus side the vegetable plants are massive, Brussel's sprouts are appearing on stalks, as are kalettes. The broccoli has arrived, showing off its spears like bonsai trees amongst the masses of leaves. I have now surpassed the world record for blanching runner beans and freezing them and I expect a representative from the Guinness Book of World Records to appear here at any moment. The tomatoes are producing lots of fruit but have decided to stay green for the time being, only allowing a few to turn dark red every now and again and of course the courgettes and marrows are planning world domination as they outnumber everything else in the garden by far. Two I lifted over the weekend were quite the largest I have ever seen and I am tempted to enter them into the Llanffas Farmers show but at £1.50 for the winner I fear the competition will be intense and a bloodbath may ensue if an infiltrator like me should win. I will keep my marrows to myself.

We have had Jo and Nicki here for the past week and for the first two days Grace, graced us with her presence. Helen has been out and about with them, letting them experience what West Wales has to offer, and despite the rain I think they have enjoyed their stay, the highlight for them being the visit from Towy Waste to empty our septic tank. They can't say we hold back on the fun here.

In addition to the weasel family, our two hedgehogs have turned into three and we are quite certain they are Mum, Dad and baby as their sizes indicate this. Mealworms are put out nightly and the wildlife camera in place to catch any activity. I do know something is also exploring the veg beds nightly as my netting is sometimes strewn across the stream bed or halfway up the garden. My guess is foxes, young ones at that; they are so playful and I think nocturnal. Frolicking with my garden netting is the highlight of their 'day'.

Our stream is showing a promise of becoming a stream again; after Sunday's downpour some water had collected in the centre which caused a slight problem as we had left the garden incinerator bin in the middle of it which resulted in Helen having to get her waterproofs on and rescue it. We needn't have worried as within a couple of hours the water had drained away and we were back to having a dry ditch once more.

Our little orchard has struggled in this summer of unpredictable weather. We had about three plums, all of which the wasps had plundered first, leaving us the holey remains. Helen had hung a jam jar with sugared water in to catch them and the result was a jar full of hornets! They were huge and a sting from them would most definitely be felt. Our apple tree on the other side of the garden though, has fared well and there will be lots to be picked once September arrives.

Did I mention the hens? No, I didn't. The hens are actually enjoying life. Every morning they are fed, watered and left to roam free amongst the vegetables, compost heap and lawns, where they can scratch around for grubs and the like to their hearts' content and we in return get absolutely zero eggs. Nothing, nada, zilch. No eggs at all. We actually bought some the other day. I am at a loss now as to what to do with these three barren chickens who are living the high life rent free. I may leave a packet of sage and onion stuffing in their run and see if that does the trick. Watch this space.

Tonight we tried out an organic weed killer on our paths and gravel drive. It is made from white vinegar, salt and washing up liquid. One gallon of vinegar mixed with a cup of salt and a tablespoonful of washing up liquid is supposed to wipe out any weed or plant for that matter and they are guaranteed not to return. Call me a cynic but I will believe it when I see (or don't) see it. The garden smells like a fish and chip shop now but at least we know we haven't harmed any wildlife in our endeavours to rid ourselves of the copious amounts of weeds that appear on our drive. If it doesn't work we will have to revert to moving the paths such is the abundant growth. Once again, watch this space.

*

The last of the visitors have left and it is a couple of weeks before we have the next friends to stay. There are so many chores to complete in the garden before then but unfortunately the sun seems to have been replaced with non-stop drizzle preventing any grass cutting or maintenance.

Next week will see the dogs bundled into the back of the car for a trip to the vets to get their booster vaccinations. Phoebe hates the car, shades of her long trip over from Zante still haunt her memory I feel as she shakes every time. Flo on the other hand loves the car and stares out of every possible window, laughing manically whilst smearing drool everywhere. The actual vet appointment scheme here is a bit haphazard with its 'turn up and get seen' system but it seems to work. Phoebe once in the surgery is very calm and allows the vet to do anything. Flo on the other hand is another matter. For some reason as soon as the vet goes to do anything she starts giving her impression of a kangaroo on speed. Everyone in the room has to chase her and pin her down. She is not nasty or anything, just a reluctant patient. *Oh, joy.*

So the marrow problem has had a small dent made in it this afternoon with four kilograms of the flipping stuff ending up in jam pots with ginger. I have to admit it does taste delicious. A further two kilograms will be made into chutney tomorrow and I think visitors may be going home clutching a few jars. We are also having to use up the defrosted fish and chicken that some complete idiot (me) caused by inadvertently pulling the wrong plug out in the garage ending up with our second freezer being switched off. Fortunately it was only the top layer that started to defrost so we have fish for the next few days and a search of the internet and our recipe books for varying recipes to stop us getting bored witless with salmon.

Yesterday Helen helped out Trevor and Jill with their endless piles of log stacking from the trees they had felled. Needless to say we won't have any need to buy logs this winter with a promise of shedfuls from them. I cooked all the workers lunch and we sat out in their 'secret garden' and enjoyed a meal together surrounded by the woodland and wildlife and their four dogs and two cats, not to mention the two sheep and dozens of chickens. I for one thoroughly enjoyed the company and banter and there is always plenty of banter with Trevor.

Apples are starting to ripen on our trees and the broccoli has been blanched and bagged and frozen. If I don't pull the wrong plug out again we should have plenty of veg to get us through most of the winter. Actually Helen has put tape on the plug in case this dipstick repeats it all over again. The tomatoes are starting to go the right colour and those that stay green will end up in some sort of chutney. The hens are completely on strike still. We thought perhaps they were laying their eggs in the garden so a reconnaissance mission was set up to try and find the secret egg-laying place. So we looked into bushes and shrubs, waded through knee-high ferns and meadowsweet flowers. Lifted up smelly compost and dug our way through mounds of grass cuttings only to find no such place existed. Just in case, we thought we would keep them in their run so if they did perchance feel like laying an egg the search area would be reduced. Nope! We are now scratching our heads even after following all the advice on the Carmarthenshire poultry keepers site. Trevor's hens are laying copious amounts of eggs, I am reliably told. However, we are now so attached to the hens we can't part with them so it looks like we have three freeloaders inhabiting the chicken house and run. So summing up, we buy all their food, grit, give them fresh veg, cook pasta and clean them regularly and they do absolutely bugger all in return. We have three adolescent hens; before we know it they will be demanding money and lifts into Llanfwr to see their mates. Knowing us two we will probably do it too.

It is starting to feel as though autumn is peeking its head above the parapet here in Wales. Not that the leaves are turning yet but there is this feel of mists and colder mornings, heavy dew and the berries are starting to appear on the trees as if to reassure the birds that some food will be available to get them through the hard months. They need not worry as we have a shed full of bird seed, meal worms and fat balls. The birds here in Ty Mawr can hardly lift themselves off the tables after the banquet we give them but boy do we have an abundance of birds. The sparrows I swear have increased weekly and the bushes move with their chattering and hopping around. I love sparrows; they are so sociable and eat everything that is given to them, strange to think they are on the decline. In London for instance, sparrow numbers fell by 60% between 1994 and 2004 and the house sparrow is now on the red list of conservation concern. The main causes are pollution and lack of invertebrates in the inner cities. The best thing you can put out for them if you do live in a city or built-up area are mealworms. Wouldn't it be just dreadful if we lost these lovely little birds forever?

CHAPTER 33

The vet visit actually passed without much incident. Phoebe as predicted was very good and Flo as predicted wasn't. She was OK with the jab but when the vet tried to shove the pipette full of kennel cough vaccine up her nose she backed into a corner, resulting in Helen having to lay on her while the vet pinned her with her free hand. The whole thing was brief though and we walked out the surgery a lot lighter in cash but relieved it was over. Phoebe threw up in the car going and coming back and Flo distanced herself as far back as she could do from the resulting mess in the boot of the Duster. Fortunately neither of them paddled through it so we were spared having to hose them down and were thankful we had bought a removable rubber boot liner!

We managed to put up shelving in the garage yesterday. This is primarily to accommodate the jars of preserves I have produced. So far marmalade, both orange and lemon, marrow and ginger jam, marrow chutney and green tomato chutney have been made and stored alongside the empty jam jars awaiting to be filled. To those of you I have promised to send some to, I am on it, I just haven't go to the point of packing it or posting it yet and chutney is always better a few weeks in, it gives it time for the flavours to mature. So be patient, you will get it. However, I have tonight found after a couple of days of feeling poorly, headache and generally out of salts, which I blamed on RA, that my left side has a shingle rash so while that is there I had better keep myself to myself. Helen is also feeling unwell and I think she has picked up a virus. She had the worst virus I have ever seen last year resulting in a perforated eardrum which has never been the same since, and she is suffering again. To get Helen to go to see the GP is comparable to trying to get a fish to recite Shakespeare. However, I will continue to nag and I'm good at it.

Life continues to be good here at Ty Mawr and finally we may find out if the farmer who owns the adjacent field to us will sell us it. It is about an acre of rough pasture leading down to the river. We both really would love it as we can plant an orchard of fruit trees, gain fishing rights, sow wildflowers and also keep the bees on it, eventually forming an apiary. The owner, however, has historically been reluctant to sell, but the estate agent has sent up a meeting with them this very evening and we feel at last we could be getting somewhere as all he has to say is 'no' and that would be the end of it. However, a meeting means negotiation and that in turn could mean 'yes'. Fingers crossed. We have decided that if we get it we may even put in a natural pond. Our whole purpose is to allow wildlife to roam free and encourage more to visit.

As far as the weather is concerned, we had a short break from rain today for about seven hours and then by the evening a massive downpour lasting at least half an hour. Having said that our stream is still not back, but I have a feeling it will not be long before we can dangle our feet in it again. The weasels haven't made any more appearances that we have noticed, but the hedgehogs come around every night for their feast; around nine o'clock each evening we can put on the outside light to see them munching away to their hearts' delight. The garden is also full of common frogs. I find myself working in the garden, perhaps pulling weeds when all of a sudden a frog will jump out, never failing to make me jump at the same time! Lastly the chickens… still no eggs. Jill turned up today with a dozen eggs for us from her brood and in exchange trotted off home with some jam and chutney. Tomorrow we have been invited up to theirs to help ourselves to eating apples, grapes for jam making, red and black currants and anything else we may need. I have to say it was quite a good feeling today making the chutney as I walked to the greenhouse and gathered up all the fallen green tomatoes, picked some red chillies, went over to the cooking apple tree and got what I needed and then went to the shed and grabbed a couple of onions and garlic bulbs and they all went into the pot after being prepared to turn into the green tomato chutney with a few more ingredients of course. I felt so satisfied and so content. I am convinced that it really is the simple things in life that give you the most pleasure.

The summer seems to have shuffled of its mortal(?) coil and a very strange season it has been although I may be speaking far too early as the weather forecasters are promising an Indian summer in September. However, not for Wales. The South East of England look like they are in for the return of the sweaty armpits and hot flushing season, whereas all we can expect is less rain, just about, if we are lucky. Looking on the bright side, or should I say dull and overcast side, we did fully expect to be rained on a lot when we moved here, so the last few weeks of uninterrupted sunshine have been a real joy and will probably have to sustain us for at least the next five years or so. Call me a cynic.

So as you may have gathered from the last paragraph it is raining, a lot, almost constantly. We have managed to garden in-between the raindrops. The courgette and marrow plants have been uprooted and deposited on the compost before they grew legs and started running amok around the garden. Beans have been tidied, broccoli cut, the sprouts are starting to form on the stalks and slowly but surely the tomatoes are turning red. I haven't made any more jams and chutneys so far but there is a queue of marrows still adorning our wood shed roof and every time I pass them a pang of guilt hits me and I find myself promising them I will put them to good use and that their lives have not been grown in vain.

As there is a definite autumnal feel now, the log fire has been lit more than once in the evenings and I must admit to actually enjoying the cosiness of the cottage. The flip-flops are not getting much attention now and I have actually worn a fleece once or twice, strange really when you think it is still only August but this summer did start early. As for the purchasing of the field next to us, the saga continues and gets a bit strange. We have commissioned the estate agent who sold the cottage to us to enquire with the owner of the field as to whether he will sell it to us or not. He promised us faithfully that he was meeting with the owner last Thursday evening and would contact us Friday morning with an answer. Nothing happened Friday morning so I phoned his office to be told he was out and that he would phone us back. He did not, so I sent him a text which he read as indicated by the 'text read' message and have since telephoned, emailed and still nothing. Bizarre! So to say we are cross would be an understatement. It's downright rude and very unprofessional. We feel like saying stuff it but I have a feeling the owner will not sell and for some reason best known to the estate agent he can't tell us. We are baffled and disappointed.

The good news is… drum roll please… one of the hens has been laying an egg every day!!! Imagine that, a chicken doing what it should do. Helen nearly fell over when she saw it lying in the hay, she staggered out of the hen house in shock clutching it in her sweaty little hand, barely able to speak. A momentous moment in the life and times of Ty Mawr. We are, however, becoming quite apathetic and if they stop laying again the most reaction we can muster I suspect, will be an eye roll and a half-hearted shrug.

If you haven't seen 'The Bodyguard' on BBC1 then do. It is a superior drama that grabs you from the very start; we can't wait for the next episode and while I am on the recommendation subject if you want a good read that will make you laugh, cry, become thoughtful and reflect then get a copy of *Not That Kind of Love* by Clare and Greg Wise. It started as a blog written by her about her journey through breast cancer and the blog was finished by her brother Greg who nursed her through her final weeks. Greg is an actor and married to Emma Thompson. It is a heartwarming, tearjerking, honest and candid account of two sides of the same story, that of the sufferer and that of the relative. Do read it, you won't regret it.

CHAPTER 34

I was the first to get up this morning and as I looked out of the bedroom window I could tell the sun was going to shine all day. As usual my first task is to let the dogs into the garden and then venture outside to let the chickens out of their hut. On my way back to the cottage I suddenly looked around me and the sight made me stop in my tracks. The daylight was not quite established, making the hills surrounding us partially silhouetted against the muted sky and the whole valley was covered in a veil of mist suspended in the air as if to delay the moment when it would be pulled back to reveal the beauty of the day in glorious technicolour. I sighed, shook my head and felt happy.

We decided to take a visit to the Farmyard Nurseries for Helen to take some more photographs for their 2019 calendar. Riding along the country lanes today on our way, I really absorbed the views and the total beauty of our surroundings.

There was an autumnal feel to the air as we strolled around the nursery grounds. It's a vast place housing at least twenty poly tunnels and has every type of plant you can think of. This time Richard the owner showed us his new carnivorous plant collection. The poly tunnel they were in was very humid and the plants were shaped like long tubes and on the edges of the top of these plants a tempting scent to lure in the insects, of which there were plenty, all lining up to meet their fate. We ended up spending far too much money but did manage to get a lovely large terracotta plant pot to place on the large tree stump we have at the end of our garden. It now sits resplendent with a hosta plant growing exuberantly out of it. Helen has transformed one of the rockery areas we have and the abundance of flowers covered in small tortoiseshell butterflies is a sight to behold.

Back home and we both went over to Trevor and Catherine's to forage for fruit and veg. We all swap a lot of our produce and homemade preserves. Today we came away with hedgerow jams, herb jelly and absolutely beautiful eating apples and Bramleys. We all sat around talking and Helen helped Trevor load his pickup with logs to take to their log store. Early evening saw us sitting around chatting some more and enjoying each other's company.

This week will see the first anniversary of our viewing this cottage. The fifth of September was the day we found it. We can't believe nine months have gone already and we are three months away from living here for a year. Where on earth does the time go? We have done so much in this short time with help from good friends and family. The kitchen has been transformed, the upstairs bathroom retiled. Pictures hung, cupboards installed, furniture rearranged. Outside fencing and gates have been erected along with the greenhouse and raised vegetable beds. Topsoil and composts put in, compost areas installed, chicken run and houses have been established and all in all after a lot of hard work we are getting there. We have learnt an awful lot too regarding keeping poultry, vegetable growing and have also learnt by our mistakes which means hopefully next year's growing season will be even more beneficial than this year. We know now what to grow and where to grow it and what will do well and what will not. Our garage freezer bought especially for our produce is full already so although the first year can be improved, we haven't done badly.

The hens have bucked their ideas up also. Today we had two eggs so that area of production is improving and to be honest I would be hard pushed to know what to do with three eggs a day.

I sat and watched the dogs playing today. They were running around our garden for ages, thoroughly enjoying themselves. They are inseparable, these two. Today we popped into Talley to buy some compost and decided to take Flo with us for a short ride as she absolutely loves the car. If I ever leave the boot open for any reason, Flo jumps into it expectantly hoping she is going on a jolly. Phoebe on the other hand, hates it and throws up five minutes into the journey. So today we thought we would give Flo a treat. We left Phoebe indoors and the cries as we shut the door were heart rending. She howled. Flo did enjoy it but the interesting thing is when we arrived home after out fifteen-minute jaunt, I let Phoebe out and she didn't run to us at all but made a beeline for Flo and they greeted each other as though they had been separated for months. Perhaps we won't do that again. Phoebe's sobs were too hard to hear. We are daft with our dogs, we fully admit it, but we wouldn't have it other way and I suspect neither would Flo and Phoebe.

Just as we had resigned ourselves to never, ever hearing about the adjoining field we are hoping to buy we had a surprise visitor. Last Sunday as both Helen and I worked in the garden an elderly, very smartly dressed lady came strolling down our lane. She stopped at our gate and introduced herself as Mrs Williams, the owner of the field! Evidently she and her husband are having just as much trouble nailing down the elusive estate agent as we have been enduring. The good news is they are more than willing to sell the field which we are over the moon about. It's about an acre and would be excellent for planting out an orchard and placing the hives on next year. The only spanner in the works now is still trying to get the agent to value it as the Willlams's only do business through him. So he is now holding everything up. We are still baffled as to his business practice and short of going into the office and bundling him in the boot of the car to value the field we are at a loss of what to do next to move this forward. Every attempt at contacting him is fruitless. *Grrrrrrrrr!*

*

I feel quite sad today as it is my mum's birthday. She would have been ninety-nine and it is the first birthday without her. The platitudes that she was a 'good age' or 'you were lucky to have her so long' mean nothing when it's your mum and your grief and loss. Irrespective of age loss is loss and hits us all in its own personal, brutal way. I will cut a rose from her 'Mum in a Million' rose bush and put it next to the picture of her taken when she was eighteen, standing in all her best clothes in black and white looking beautiful, the rest of her long life stretching before her, unknown to her then, known to me now. She really wanted her telegram from the Queen and if it hadn't been for the fall she had and the subsequent injuries she suffered, I truly believe she may have made it but instead she has gone and every day I say, 'Morning Mum,' to the rose bush that her ashes have been placed under, smile during the day when a memory comes to mind or sometimes cry when the missing gets a little too much. Anyway, happy birthday, Mum, wherever you are.

CHAPTER 35

We had a lovely week with Carol and Steve. As usual Steve attended to lots of little jobs for us, moving bathroom cabinets and mirrors, mowing lawns, assembling bee hives and sorting out my thermostatic windows for the greenhouse that they bought me for my birthday. In addition to all of this he mended the cigar lighter in my car which I needed for my sat nav. The man is a genius. Carol, another genius in her own right, mended one of my favourite jumpers that Phoebe had clawed in her efforts to climb up me when she greeted me after a long period of separation lasting all of fifteen minutes when I left her indoors to go into the garden to feed the birds. I love that about dogs, they give you the biggest welcome even if you have only been to the loo. That's if they haven't actually joined you, of course. Having dogs is like having toddlers, you don't bath or shower alone or go to the loo by yourself. You are in great danger of tripping over them as they are constantly under your feet and you can't leave anything laying around in case they choke on it.

Anyway, back to Carol; she also turned my poncho cape into a poncho cape that won't slip off your shoulders and end up on the floor behind you. We also took a trip to Dinefwr and spent a lovely hour listening and interrupting a talk on fashions of the 17th Century. It was quite fascinating and informative, especially finding out that ladies didn't wear knickers in those days. We came out very grateful for the liberating garb we are now able to wear, not to mention the knickers.

*

Sad news. Gertie, one of our hens, has disappeared. Yesterday I went out to feed them their usual warm spaghetti at around 11 o'clock and only Gladys and Edna greeted me. At this time in the morning this is not unusual as the hens tend to lay their eggs in their house around late morning, so I thought nothing of it, assuming Gertie was brooding in the hen house, however, later in the afternoon Helen was having one of her usual natters over the back fence with Trevor when they heard a lot of noise coming from the chickens in the back of our garden. As this sometimes does happen neither of them were particularly worried but when bedtime came for the chickens only Gladys and Edna were there. We both searched the garden frantically, looking in hedges and shrubs, greenhouses and anywhere we thought she could be hiding but she could not be found. Chickens don't wander off on their own; if one goes to the other field the others follow in quick succession. Our theory is, due to the lack of feathers, that a buzzard or peregrine may have swooped down and grabbed her. Failing that, a fox has made a very clean kill, but this seems less likely to me as foxes do tend to leave a trail of carnage in their wake.

Trevor has told us she may still return as sometimes hens do go off alone and brood for about two days then wander back as though nothing has happened. We will have to see. I hope he is right but feel she may be gone for good. We both feel quite sad but take solace in the fact that our chickens have a lovely life roaming free and feeding well. It has made us wary of letting the other two out as if it was a predator it may well return knowing that an easy dinner is available. Wherever you are, Gertie, we miss you and thank you for the lovely eggs you gave us.

Although it is still relatively warm for September, as it is Wales it is raining, all day, every day, days without end. We do have the most spectacular green grass though, no wonder Tom Jones sang about it. We are busy trying to tidy up the garden at the moment in between the periods of torrential rain. The runner beans need disassembling and putting on the compost heap along with all the other defunct plants. We have now frozen all the cauliflowers, beans, peas, broad beans etc. The Brussel's sprouts are doing well and getting ready to pick. The celeriac is staying in the ground and just dug up when we need it. This is the crop I am most pleased about as it is notoriously hard to grow anything bigger than a golf ball and we have managed a small bowling ball size with a wonderful taste. I have planted the late potatoes and the winter onions and garlic has yet to go in. When our wet suits and snorkels arrive from Amazon I am sure we will feel equipped to venture out and plant them. Wish us luck.

*

Gertie has come home to roost, so to speak. Jokes about being out on a hen night, having an eggceptional time, etc., etc. have been banded around ad infinitum but the truth is we haven't a clue where she went. She was very wet when she turned up and headed straight for the food in the pen. The other two didn't seem very delighted to see her, not one champagne cork popped, no welcome home banners nor from what I could gather even a hello hug. I have to say Helen and I were over the moon that she came back unharmed and we are now getting two eggs a day again so the cake-making has resumed, as have the boiled egg breakfasts. So that is one Ty Mawr mystery that remains unsolved but had a happy hending...

The weather is atrocious. We have fifty-mile-an-hour winds and torrential rain. Our stream is full to overflowing and we have spent the morning picking up broken tree branches, windfall apples and generally clearing up the dishevelment that Mother Nature has wreaked. The river fortunately hasn't broken its banks and is thankfully fast-flowing so it drains away fairly quickly, however nearer to Carmarthenshire the river has reached the main road which is concerning for those living nearby. Ty Mawr was built in 1860 and thus far no flooding has occurred and let's hope it stays that way.

We finally met the gentleman who owns the field, a wily old chap with a twinkle in his eye and a great, dry sense of humour. He is getting it valued, as are we, and hopefully we can come to a mutually agreeable price and the field will be ours. We feel hopeful that it will happen after having met the owner and his wife so fingers crossed. He asked where I was from and when I said the East End of London he said he was so sorry... It did make me laugh and he had a wry smile on his face.

We have had a busy couple of days trying to sort out the vegetable gardens and 'putting to bed' some of the old crops. The winter potatoes are making their appearance as are the wonderful Brussel's sprouts, so Christmas dinner is getting there! I still have the winter garlic and onions to plant and hopefully I can keep our salad leaves growing all the time in the greenhouse. The weather as mentioned isn't allowing us to do a lot of outdoor jobs so today Helen decided we would finally get the bureau out of the shed and put it in the conservatory. The first problem was clearing enough of the junk that was in front of it away; after a lot a pushing and shoving, moaning and groaning we finally got out of our armchairs and headed for the shed. It was actually a lot easier than we had thought and now the bureau has been cleaned and polished to within an inch of its life and looks rather good. It is still full of everything we don't need and never have needed but according to Helen 'it all might come in handy one day'.

I did get Helen cheesed off today though. She decided to go to the builders' merchant to buy some Polyfilla for all the holes that have been left by our moving cupboards, etc. I asked her to get me a box of masonry nails while she was there which immediately threw her into a tizzy because she didn't know what size to get. Confidently I told her they only do one size only to find when she came home that she had gone through the equivalent of the Spanish inquisition as to what size she required! Fortunately she came home with the right ones due to common sense but a minor telling off transpired. Guilty as charged but as I pointed out we have both learnt something today at least. It didn't go down as well as I hoped.

We are still going to do a car boot sale with all the stuff that won't come in handy one day. This car boot adventure has been in the planning now for about seven years so when it happens it should be sensational, in fact less planning went into the invasion of Dunkirk. We have got as far as buying a table on which to place the assortment of stuff we don't need which includes several odd-shaped plastic food containers, light shades that were quite popular in 1972, dozens of picture frames with A4 photographs that Helen and I took when we first got our cameras and thought they were good but in retrospect they are only OK, and the list goes on. Assorted cutlery, kitchenware and of course the obligatory CDs, DVDs and books. When and if this momentous day does occur I will actually believe in miracles until then I will just believe it when I see it.

'Ode to Autumn' by John Keats is one of my all-time favourite poems that sums up this time of year so succinctly.

As I look out of the windows here in Ty Mawr the sun throws out that gentle warmth that only an autumn sun can, the blue sky interspersed with tiny fluffy white clouds stretches on and on as I look down the valley and the trees struggle to stay green as the edges of their leaves start to turn into a burnt orange, red or yellow adding to the colour of the garden as only autumn can. There isn't a season I do not like, really, each one for me has its own benefits, and living here and experiencing the seasons in West Wales for the first time brings with it new discoveries and changing landscapes. We wake up every morning to a heavy mist hanging over the ground, the valley blanketed in this shroud of white, swirling, ghost-like haze muffling the sounds of nature until the sun is strong enough to disperse it to whence it came only to return in the evening and spend another night adding stillness to the surrounding area.

The days have been beautiful, unremitting sunshine. We have been busy as usual in our gardens. Helen has planted all her spring bulbs of which there were many. We will have the joy of watching them break through the cold ground left by winter once the spring starts to rouse the earth out of its wintertime slumber. She has added to the already abundant daffodils, planted more tulips, alliums and crocus and no doubt has more plans to further the colours of the Ty Mawr garden. For my part of the garden the winter onions and garlic have been planted and the winter cabbage is on standby to go into a bed soon. The vegetable garden keeps on giving and the salad leaves and tomatoes are still making us eat healthily. I have made some more green tomato chutney but this time with the emphasis on garlic to ensure a different taste. I am seriously thinking of having a produce stall before Christmas at one of the little Christmas fayres that the villages surrounding us have, but have no idea what to charge. Any advice is welcome.

We have actually tackled some of the four and half million boxes in the garage full of stuff (OK, slight exaggeration but believe me, it feels like four and a half million). We spent Wednesday in the garage going through each box and sorting out what is to be kept and what is to be sold. The box of our Christmas decorations had been invaded by squatting mice. Helen's nativity stable had lent itself to a mouse nest made up of tinsel and cotton wool with some shredded wire from the fairy lights thrown in, no doubt to add to the festive fun going on in there. It actually looked like the mice had a better Christmas than we did and at least they didn't have to watch The Sound of Music and The Great Escape as there was no television there, or if there was they had shredded it. I wonder how many mice babies were born in that particular stable, I should guess quite a few going by the copious amounts of mouse poo and urine. Needless to say we need another nativity set.

Helen's father Owen, it has to be said, left a fair amount of tools. There are hundreds of various tools to be had, some are unused, some date back to at least the 1930s. We got Trevor down to take his pick of anything he wanted and also to tell us what some of them were used for. He went home clutching a bench grinder and bench clamp and very happy he looked too.

We have sorted only about half of the contents and so far there is quite a lot of items that we can car boot. Neither of us have any idea what to charge and to have to scroll through somewhere like eBay to try and get an idea would take an age so I am going to guesstimate and hope for the best. I hate selling at these events. The minute you · arrive, park your car and start to unload you are descended upon by the other 'car booters', seasoned traders and dealers who can smell a bargain at fifty yards and will try to get you off guard as you attempt to unpack. Nightmare! I may take the dogs and let them loose on the marauding mob to see if their persistent crotch-sniffing will put them off. Fingers crossed.

CHAPTER 36

The past few days have been interesting and entertaining. We started off with attending a Macmillan coffee morning at the church hall in Talley. We had never been to the hall before but we turned up armed with an apple and sultana cake and some books for the mini library and got a lovely welcome and by the end of the morning the little hall was packed to the rafters. We all managed to raise in excess of £215, not bad for a tiny village. We also met some lovely people there including another same-sex couple who have a smallholding nearby so we are not the only gays in the village! Everyone was so friendly and we had fun in addition to learning a lot about local tradesmen and various other get-togethers that are available. It is nice to be part of a community, especially one that really does look out for one another. On the Facebook page for the village, if someone needs a lift into Llanfwr or anywhere local they just ask on the page and someone offers to pick them up and bring them back. If you are poorly someone will do your shopping, if you want anything cheap or free you can ask and I guarantee someone will know someone who can help out. It's a restorative in human nature.

Helen left to go back to Sussex for a couple of days and then on to London to celebrate Jenny's birthday this weekend, so I am here alone at the moment. It's funny but the dogs are not settled when one of the 'pack' are away. They constantly look out the windows and if a car does come along our lane they seem to be convinced it is

Helen and go into an excited frenzy. I do feel for them even though clearly I am not sufficient company! They also think it is a perfect excuse to get on the bed in the night, just in case I feel lonely I suppose. I do wake up in strange positions, accommodating them, and have to unfold myself on waking in order to actually stand up. Flo also gets on the couch next to me and gets as close as she possibly can; she is a complete and utter baby. Phoebe is far less dependent on humans due I suspect to the degree of self-preservation she had to have to survive in Greece, so she sleeps quite soundly in front of the fire unless of course she fancies having her chest stroked and then she won't stop pestering me until I stroke her. I am definitely convinced dogs have sussed out human beings (some) and monopolise entirely on how stupid we are, and Helen and I fit into the stupid category really well.

Last night I went over to Trevor and Catherine's house. As it was Catherine's birthday they had invited me over for a takeaway Indian meal. Dear Trevor drove forty minutes each way to Lampeter to get it and after putting it in the Aga for about ten minutes it emerged piping hot and delicious. We had a really great time and Trevor never fails to make me laugh until my stomach hurts. The banter between him and Jill is so funny and we have agreed Trevor could never get a job in the diplomatic service or volunteer for the Samaritans. The man, lovely as he is, just says whatever enters his head. I am informed by Jill it is because there is nothing in his head to stop it! I will give you some examples. According to Trevor, Helen and I have come here to die, we are the two silly cows up the road, I must have been quite nice looking before I got old and do I want Catherine's mum's four wheeled Zimmer frame, adding that it does have a basket on it (for some reason he feels I would be really tempted by that accessory). I could go on and on. Jill holds her head in her hands and stares at the floor and I think she is relieved I just howl with laughter at his comments.

I did sit at their table last night feeling absolutely blessed that we do have such nice, good neighbours who have made our transition into rural living so much easier and have helped us no end. I have to admit I found it alien at first to have so much attention from people I didn't know too well but now ten months into our life here, I truly appreciate it.

The weather here is wet again, no surprises really, however, I have to admit there is something very comforting and cosy about lighting the wood burner in the afternoon and pottering about indoors for a change as there is still plenty to do. We had to have a carpenter in today as our back door has gone rotten with rain at the bottom. This is a heavy-duty oak cottage door and is lovely, so we were gutted it looked so poorly. I always send photos of whatever needs attention to Steve via Carol and he advises and always offers to mend whatever it is the next time they come, another blessing for us, those two, but in this case we felt we should get it attended to promptly before it got any worse. Fortunately the carpenter is going to repair it; by the sounds of it he does this around here often. He will take the door away leaving us with a plywood sheet for a couple of days and make the door like new again and replace the door frame as it is affected also. So that turned out better than we hoped.

Ty Mawr was severely affected by Storm Callum.

We were sleeping soundly when something hit our bedroom window. Helen jumped out of bed to find Trevor standing on our lawn telling us to get out as a flood was approaching. By the time we gathered our wits together the conservatory floor started to fill with water. Literally before we could get out the door the whole of the downstairs was under at least twelve inches of water and we had to leave by the back of the house. The water was brown and dirty and swirling around us causing quite a current. One of the lasting memories I have is of one of my Sainsbury's slippers floating past me with only the little blue bow on it showing.

Helen, Louise and I and the two dogs waded and doggy paddled respectively through the flood and currents to get to the front gate where it was dry as the ground is slightly higher up. This experience was hideous and frightening to say the least. It was pitch black with no electricity and the only place we could go was to Trevor and Catherine's.

We bedded the dogs down in the back of the car in Trevor's garden and all went indoors to watch the river becoming higher and higher and heading its way towards their house. We never slept, we were wet and cold and exhausted and I would not wish this on my worst enemy. The night was long and wet and dark and seemed to go on and on forever. Water then started to seep into Trevor's living room and we went out the back of his house to find his garden room awash, as the small area outside it was flooded now too.

By dawn we could see the devastating effects and extent of the flood. The whole of our garden both back and front was covered in water that came above our knees. We went down to the cottage to find the ground floor awash as before but the water level higher. Nothing was spared. Rugs, sofas, white goods, boiler, tables, chairs, electrical equipment – the list goes on.

Helen and I waded through what was our home, our warm, cosy, familiar, lovely home and neither of us spoke a word. Now and again one of us would stoop to pick something familiar out of the dark brown water, a shoe, some documents, a pillow, one of the dogs' toys. Water is so destructive and unrelenting. It gushes into every part of your home leaving nothing in its wake. It rips into wood, plaster, wool, fabric, it spares nothing.

Then there was the garden, the garage, the shed, the wood shed and the greenhouse. Everything in them floating and bobbing on the surface, even the chest freezer. This sort of thing happens to other people on the news, not us, surely?

We managed to be able to stay in the holiday let on the estate that was unaffected by the flood, which was a blessing. Of course being a Saturday our insurers were shut and we had to wait until Monday before we could find out what help we would be available. By Sunday the water level had receded and we could see the grass again and our home was left with just a thick brown silt-like covering. We spent Sunday on our hands and knees in thick mud scrubbing and cleaning and getting the floor to a point where we would not slip and slide around on it. It was by no means clean but it was recognisable and made us feel a bit better. The community offered a lot of help but we were aware that we should try and leave as much of the destruction for the risk assessor to see, but what an amazing group of people we have living near us.

Poor Louise was so good, ensuring the dogs were kept company and entertained while we spent our time in what was left of our home. I have promised her a better holiday next time!

So Monday came and the phone calls were made and the insurers were great. An electrician was sent out to get the power back on, a team of 'drying out' experts was promised which only amounted to one young man who couldn't drive his large van to save his life and hit our fence post, denting his vehicle, but by this time Helen and I were so numb and deflated we didn't even bat an eyelid. So at least we had power, the dehumidifiers were switched on and running, great big monsters in the living room, kitchen and landing. They look like something H G Wells had conjured up in a sci-fi novel, their large silver corrugated tentacles reaching out across each room like space-age squid washed up on a beach.

To date we are waiting for the boiler to be replaced, the rooms to dry out, and the electrician to come tomorrow to finish repairing the electrics. We have a team of people coming to assess the furniture to see what is salvageable and can be deep cleaned and what will end up in the skip. We also have another team in to clean the house for us to ensure the residue of the silt is gone. We have to have all our skirting boards replaced, the walls cleaned, the whole of the kitchen cabinets replaced and possibly the oven. The dishwasher, washing machine and tumble dryer are also defunct. I could go on and on, not forgetting the gravel in the garden needs replacing and the greenhouse is full of rubbish including someone's apple harvest that found its way in there. Helen had lost one of her posh wellies and actually walked down to the end of the river where it turns and found it despite Louise and I telling her she never would and that it was halfway to Ireland by now. It's going to take months to get our home back to where it was but on the positive side we didn't like the colour of the cooker, the kitchen units were tired and past their best and we had flood insurance. The other silver lining is that once again the planning officer demanded yet another pedantic piece of information and a further diagram of our proposed works but when he learned of our circumstance her waived the bureaucracy and said he would push everything through. Result, but at quite a hefty cost so we are not celebrating really.

Both Louise and I have had bad dreams since the weekend. Louise dreamt she was back in the flood and woke up in a panic and I dreamt it was raining hard and likewise woke up in the same state. Helen has spent restless nights tossing and turning and sitting on the side of the bed unable to sleep. So events like this are not to be underestimated, they play on your psyche and although you feel you have coped and come through and managed well it actually can stick with you and rear its ugly, wet head when you least expect it.

CHAPTER 37

I think when all this mayhem first happened Helen and I summoned up our best 'Dunkirk' spirit and decided to forge ahead regardless. However, day six and the stiff upper lip has become decidedly quivery and many tears have been shed; some angry outbursts have been known to happen but overwhelming sadness has probably beaten the rest of our emotions into a cocked hat.

Helen sifted through her document drawer which unfortunately was in the bottom of the bureau in the conservatory. Birth, death and marriage certificates, passports, her baby book and dozens upon dozens of photographs all ruined. Birthday cards or just cards written by past friends, her mum, dad and sister all among the ruined ink- and water-stained pile of papers that now lay on the floor of the conservatory. Memories and artefacts that can never, ever, be replaced, all gone in an hour by an unforgiving stream of dirty brown water that destroyed all in its wake. All of my paperwork is kept upstairs so I was fortunate in that department.

Our mood is not good, we want to leave one minute and then just make Ty Mawr wonderful again the next. We hate Wales, then we love it. We feel hopeless and then empowered. We run a gauntlet of emotions within an hour and then start all over again.

The insurance company that started off with promise has waned in its enthusiasm. Our loss adjuster still hasn't visited due to having to go on 'training days'. I must admit I sarcastically asked if it was to learn about customer care and empathy but it was wasted on him and he proceeded to explain what it was about. But the initial cleaning has taken place with two men from Birmingham spraying everything with sanitiser. They took out all our furniture which now sits at the front of our cottage and it all stands as a reminder to us every time we go out there or look out the window that our home is no more.

Strangely the one thing that really got to me was the loss of all my frozen vegetables. The veg I had grown and lovingly, proudly prepared and froze all gone to waste. I was so looking forward to serving them all up on Christmas Day. Daft but it really stung.

So we have yet another weekend of waiting to find out what the loss adjuster will say and when we can start rebuilding our lives again. We take very little pleasure at the moment in a lot of things but are heartened that our hedgehogs survived and are feeding nightly. The birds in the garden oblivious to our plight still love our feeders and the hens are still laying, albeit only one egg a day. Helen had a lovely moment last evening whilst fetching in the last of the washing that we had laundered at the holiday let, a barn owl flew by, just feet away, and landed in the tree just past our dovecote. I like to think it was tiny apology from Mother Nature to say sorry for the past few days, however, I think it should be us who apologise to her given the climate change we have created with our industries, pollution and gases that have contributed to altering what would probably have been an eternal, constant, enduring environment if we had just left it alone.

*

The 'condemned' items have now gone to meet their maker in a back of a white van; there was so much stuff the men had to come back for a second trip. It was a mixture of relief and sadness when the van finally drove off. Relief because we do not have to look at the dishevelment that was our home and sadness because we can't look at it anymore.

It rained on Friday, quite heavily, and I found Helen on more than one occasion in the conservatory staring at the sky almost willing it to stop in case another flood occurred. It's like a post-traumatic stress response, actually it is a post-traumatic stress response. The sound of the rain started to bring back dreadful memories of wading through knee-high water in pitch darkness feeling completely powerless.

However, the rain passed as normal rain does and we are back to sunny autumnal days and frost.

We have had the insurance compensation money through which has allowed us to start purchasing our white goods back. Today we took delivery of a dishwasher and tumble dryer. We have also ordered our sofas which will be with us before Christmas so we can at least sit on something more comfortable. I cleaned the last of the kitchen cupboards today to rid us of the vile silt and next week we have a surveyor to come and visit us to assess the building's damage. We fully expect to be in a pickle until at least February but are buoyed on by the promise of the cottage looking even better by then than it was before.

Helen and I are finally sleeping better at night and we have taken residence in the living room instead of living upstairs. We have two swivel chairs that straddle the Orwellian squid-like machine and the TV is up and running. As long as we have the volume up to a dangerous level to overcome the constant droning of the squid machine we can watch and hear said TV, however, Helen's already compromised hearing is being challenged to its limits which was demonstrated the other day by her insisting that a character in Poirot was called 'Shitole'. She was so adamant I had to Google the cast list of characters and then replay that scene; it transpired the woman hadn't said her name at all but merely said in response to a question, 'She died?' Perhaps a visit to the audiology department is needed.

I ventured into the greenhouse the other day and my spirits did plummet even further. The tomato plants looked dreadful; the bark chippings on the floor had been pushed into a heap on one side covering the plants there. The whole greenhouse smelt awful. I am going to have to clear it all and then power wash the glass etc. for it to be clean and used next spring. I just can't face the effort at present.

Trevor and Jill arrived on our doorstep both dressed as Captain Birdseye to power wash our paths and gravel. We were grateful for this as our power washer was no more and had gone on a jolly in the back of the white van. It was a good job done as the layers of grey, muddy silt kept being traipsed indoors every time we went outside.

I also forgot, after reminding absolutely everyone, to put our clocks back last night and spent the first half hour of the day thinking I had got up really late until the penny dropped. It is going to be strange now with the dark nights ascending by five o'clock. Winter is truly upon us and we are approaching our first year anniversary here. Going back over the events of last year I think I am surpassing any previous scores on the Holmes and Rahe stress scale. The loss of a parent, moving home, the flood and not forgetting the time I ran out of tea bags has got to push me over the top of it. I must take the test and see. Going to go now as I have to order a straitjacket off eBay to be delivered as soon as possible.

*

Well, we are still here, that's a positive… I think. We had the loss adjusters visit along with our claims manager Aaron. The loss adjuster's name was Katie and she was very nice. She and Aaron wandered around the dishevelment that was our home and agreed to all the losses and even found some more lurking in the garage. Katie went home clutching a jar of my homemade marmalade and I think that may have clinched a successful outcome!

Also in the mix this week will be the 'Clearaway Rubbish and House Clearance Disposal Operatives'. They are actually coming tomorrow to rid us of the grim reminder that most of our downstairs and its contents are now officially condemned. It will be good to get rid of that assorted pile of furniture, black sacks, shoes, CDs, book etc. as wherever you sit in the house you can see it, apart from the loo of course.

Then a man named Nick arrived to see what could be restored furniture-wise. He made notes and took photos; I have to say this home and its contents have now been photographed so much I am expecting *Hello* magazine to phone for exclusive rights! Anyway, back to Nick; he casually informed us that they would be taking away all of the remaining furniture which includes our table and chairs, sideboard, bookcases and all the contents therein to be 'deep cleaned' and 'sanitised'. He also cheerfully remarked we wouldn't have them back by Christmas as they are very busy at the moment due to a recent flooding… I'm so glad he informed us of this as we were oblivious to it.

So Christmas, for what it's worth, is cancelled this year and to compound that announcement we found our sopping wet artificial Christmas tree in the garage when we decided to brace ourselves and throw out all of the 'condemned' items that were in it. In addition the whole of the kitchen has to be ripped out and re-plastered, decorated and new units to go in. All the walls downstairs have to be re-plastered, also replacement skirting boards as they have all been jemmied off to allow drying. Oh, and by the way, on the drying front the dehumidifiers are working very well, so much so they are sucking every single bit of moisture going; even Helen and I on waking can't blink! I'm sure I have more wrinkles either due to the stress of it all or any moisture I did have left in my skin has been deposited in the dehumidifiers to be lost forever. We have been told they may be able to take them away in a week or so which will be a relief and means the building surveyor can visit to assess the rest of the building's damage.

Back to our non-event, AKA Christmas. We have decided one of three things. 1. Go away to a cottage in Pembrokeshire for the week, 2. Go out for Christmas dinner, or 3. Stay here and have our Christmas dinner off a trestle table providing the new cooker is here. I think I am plumping for number three at this moment in time because as disorganised as Ty Mawr is and is going to get a lot worse, I still want to be in my own home and watch Christmas crap on the tele, eating all the stuff you only eat at Christmas. Mind you I never did like dates and I think I am the only person I know who eats the perfumed Turkish delight that comes in a round balsa wood box. So I will let you know what momentous decision we arrive at but I think it will be dependent on how far the house restoration has got.

On the bright side Helen is satiating her retail desires by looking at sofas and kitchens and all the other things we need. We have been promised a pay-out for contents this Friday but the cynic in me isn't holding its breath.

All in all we are keeping our spirits up and just getting on. Once the rubbish is removed we can jet wash the awful silt that remains on our paths etc. and stop trooping it through the cottage every time we go outside. Mind you the dogs have done their fair share of spreading it around also. We can also hopefully start replacing our items one by one; the first one on the list is the dishwasher so I can get some kitchenware cleaned thoroughly and this will be closely followed by a hard floor cleaner/vacuum. Amongst the items in the garage was a huge suitcase full of my winter clothes, so a new wardrobe this coming year is not only a must-have but an absolute essential. I've decided a wet suit and snorkel in lime green would suit.

CHAPTER 38

The dehumidifiers are gone. They left this home yesterday after having done a sterling job of drying out the floor, walls, woodwork and our skin. It is a relief that yet another stage of this chapter in our flood experience has been reached and next week will see the contractors and the surveyors in to assess what needs doing and how much it will cost to do it. Silence reigns again here at Ty Mawr; the constant whirring and occasional banging of the space-age squids are no more.

Helen likened our experience regarding the flood to a deep bruise, at first it really hurts and is large and black but as the weeks go by the bruise starts to lessen and the colour lightens and the pain subsides. I like that analogy, I think at the moment the bruise is still tender and it's still obvious but it is getting better and one day we will forget how much it hurt and what a mark it left.

We have been busy replacing some items that we have lost, things like the lawnmower, sewing machine, sofas, cooker etc. Not all have arrived yet; the cooker will be with us in the next couple of weeks, the sofas December, but bit by bit we are rebuilding the material side of our home. What seems to have gone though is our love for this place. The thrill of being here has left us, either temporarily or permanently, we are not certain. I find Helen on Right Move a lot and I am struggling to go into my garden and greenhouse. My enthusiasm has gone, I have lost my mojo.

In practical terms we are applying for a government grant to help us install flood barriers to protect our home from any future flooding. If your home has been flooded by natural causes then you automatically qualify for this help. On another side we are now faced with the real possibility of the saleability of this place declining given the risk it poses. So the dream as was, is no more. Well, at the moment anyway. Every day we work to clean. I had to buy a new vacuum cleaner and the evidence that the silt remains is remarkable. The whole of the inside of the vacuum, the see-through cylinder bit, is clogged up with this fine light brown dust that resembles the consistency of talcum powder. I have steam cleaned the lower ground floors three times now and still it remains. Goodness only knows what our lungs look like. However, we keep reminding ourselves how fortunate we are to have the insurance we did and the fact that actually this is nuts and bolts stuff and we and the dogs are OK, physically at least. The emotional trauma and mental effects will probably persist for a while but even they are reasonably mild in comparison to what a lot of folk have to endure.

*

So November is here already, bringing the frost and the wind and dare I say it, the rain. I have never been so worried about the weather forecasts before now but nightly both of us are glued for the duration. November has never been my favourite month, every year when it comes around I am reminded of the poem by Thomas Hood called 'November' which I always feel sums it up succinctly and starts with the lines:

No sun – no moon!

No morn – no noon –

No dawn – no dusk – no proper time of day.

However, with the non-existent climate change; non-existent according to President Orange; November may soon be seeing us donning our shorts and sunglasses and we hurtle inexorably into the self-fulfilling prophecy of not only wiping out the human race but taking every other life form with us.

So as you may have gathered, spirits are low but we will get over this and move on in whatever direction we are led in the future.

However, this time next year may see us in a completely different place, mind-wise, that is, and the love that we had for Ty Mawr and its charms will have returned.

We started off this week with a little bit of hope that all would go well with the insurance surveyor on Monday. Most of our future plans for the house depend on his evaluation of the damage that has been caused by the flood.

We had met him before when he came to look at the storm damage and felt unimpressed with him then as he blamed the storm damage (same night) to the roof on 'wear and tear', awarding us nothing. However, forever the optimists we hoped the flood damage spoke for itself.

In addition to the obvious damage to the walls, kitchen and everything on the ground floor up to about a metre, there was the cesspit and the conservatory floor. He dismissed the conservatory floor as not being related to the flood, even though we stressed that this had never occurred before and therefore must be caused in some way by the water. As for the cesspit, he will send out a specialist in surveying these structures, so we are no nearer settling at the moment. He was definitely a 'company man'. It amazes me that as one human being to another he had no empathy for our situation. To him it was just another job and he was out to save his company as much money as possible. I understand that some people do put in fraudulent claims but in an obvious claim such as ours surely there should be some other considerations? Obviously not.

Then on Tuesday we had the 3D image of the kitchen that we had been promised by Howdens to go and see. Jill came with us as we planned to go into Carmarthen and shop for other things. We got there at the appointed time, only to find he hadn't even started the project! No apologies, nothing, but he said if we waited an hour and a half he could get it done. We walked out and went into B&Q where a lovely young man gave us all the time in the world and we got the kitchen we wanted at a fraction of the price. So out of something bad came something good. We can't order yet as the surveyor's report has to go in and the surveyor assured us it would be there by Friday. But at least we know what we can have and are happy with it.

The week rolled on with a chap from Llanfwr coming on Wednesday to price up a new conservatory for us and he was so helpful and seemingly not out for every penny he could get, and seemed to have genuine empathy for us with our predicament. He is coming back to us with a quote which includes a flood door.

The weather has turned for the time being from a soggy, damp, drizzle to sunshine, which is a relief. The river level has gone down as has the stream in the garden and that makes us feel a little more secure for now. I actually went out to inspect what was left of the vegetable garden and tidied it up and must admit to getting the old feeling of satisfaction I had before, so I am sure with time and the advent of spring and summer all will be well again. We also took delivery of a new Range cooker to replace the waterlogged one and would you believe it, when they lifted it water still came out of it!

Thursday saw us both feeling quite unwell with some sort of virus. Helen had an earache and felt 'fluey' as did I, but my head was my worst problem – continuous thumping on one side ended up driving me to bed for the most of Friday and Saturday and missing out on Trevor's birthday meal tonight as I felt far too poorly to join them all. Helen felt well enough to go, thank goodness, but I am so upset I could not join them all as we bought a cake for him and balloons. The law of sod strikes again.

So next week we are hoping to get an offer which is acceptable so we can start the rebuilding and decorating and finally get our home back; it all feels desolate at the moment with constant remnants of the destruction around us.

This time last year, tomorrow in fact, I lost my beautiful mum. Not a day goes by without wishing I could hold her, kiss her cheek, bring her flowers and make her laugh. Wherever you are, Mum, I wish you were here.

*

Finally, we have nearly concluded our negotiations with the insurance company and reached a satisfactory (we think) sum to enable us to start the repair of Ty Mawr.

Today saw the start of the reparations. Andrew arrived at 8:30am along with three other men – Sam, Simon and another whose name escapes me. They worked all day, drilling, chipping, sawing and banging things. I took refuge in the bedroom with the dogs while Helen went to Carmarthen to get her hair cut and finalise our new kitchen. I didn't realise how clever the B&Q kitchen people are. They have this shared programme that they send you the link for and between them and us we design the kitchen online and a list of what is needed is then generated and voila! A brand-new kitchen is born. So all in all very pleased with the whole set-up.

It's all very strange for us at the moment, not only can we both remember exactly what we were doing this time last year, we are almost replicating it. This time last year my mum had just died. I found that one really difficult, surprisingly so. Grief is very unpredictable; just when you think you are on top of it, it rears its ugly head and smacks you right between the eyes all over again. I thought I was doing quite well and I think I know why I thought I was doing quite well; we moved, we had all the newness of here, the garden, the neighbours, the wildlife and the weather! This all occupied my mind and put grief on the back burner, but with the flood and the consequent wrangling with insurance companies and contractors and dealing with living in a mess my theory is that finally my brain went into overload and with the advent of the anniversary of Mum's passing my head exploded, theoretically speaking of course, and to use an unfortunate parlance… the floodgates opened and I found myself a bit lost for a while. Or putting it another way… for a while in bits.

However, the replication of last year continues with us having to pack everything into boxes while Sam, Simon and the other one smash up all the bad bits that were flood damaged and replace them with shiny new bits. We have decided to do all the decorating ourselves to save some money towards the conservatory; it only involves slapping emulsion on the walls, so Helen and I are up for that.

Oddly enough both of us are excited about Christmas this year, even though we will be on our own. Well, apart from Christmas Eve when we will be having all of the neighbours in for food and drinks. I think this is because most of our Christmas decorations floated away in October and since then we have started to buy some really lovely vintage ones that are reminiscent of the 1950s; in other words they ones we grew up with. Nothing wrong with a bit of nostalgia, it connects you to memories, emotions and that feeling of family that once was. You can buy anything on eBay, even vintage Christmas wrapping paper, not a reproduction but the real McCoy. Makes you wonder what relics from the past still lurk under people's beds or on top of their wardrobes that may one day bring back a memory once lost but now rediscovered.

So that's about it for now. We celebrate our first anniversary at Ty Mawr on the 6th December, and what a year it has been. I am sure like us you all say, 'Thank goodness that's over,' when the 1st of January comes around, but this year I really mean it!

About The Author

Elizabeth Larkswood was born and raised in East London but near enough to Epping Forest to kindle her passion for the countryside and nature.

With her three young children she relocated to Suffolk and pursued a nursing career, training to be a registered nurse.

Raised in the 1950s, although she was sure of her sexuality, the times did not lend to her 'coming out' but after divorcing she decided to no longer live a lie and 'just be herself'.

Printed in Great Britain
by Amazon